| WORKBOOK & GUIDE |

CONSCIOUS MARKETING

Marketing From the Inside Out

Gain the clarity and confidence needed to
attract the clients you most want to work with

PAULETTE RAO, MCC, BCC

D0869359

N TRUE NORTH RESOURCES, LLC

CONSCIOUS MARKETING:
Marketing from the Inside Out.

For information: Paulette Rao, MCC, BCC, True North Resources LLC, 72 68th Street, Brooklyn, New York, 11220, (718) 833-5586, paulette@truenorthresources.com.

Table of Contents

Acknowledgments. vii

Preface. ix

How to Use This Guide. xiii

MODULE 1: *Ready, Set, Learn!*. 1

MODULE 2: *What Is Conscious Marketing?*. 21

MODULE 3: *How the Conscious Marketing™ System Works* 29

MODULE 4: *Identify the Self-Limiting Mindsets That Hold You Back* 37

MODULE 5: *Creating New Mindsets* 51

MODULE 6: *Connecting to Your Vision* 65

MODULE 7: *Identifying Your Favorite People to Work With*. 75

MODULE 8: *Determining Your Niche*. 83

MODULE 9: *Communicating Your Brand* 91

MODULE 10: *What Problems Do You Solve?*. 103

MODULE 11: *What Solutions Do You Bring to Bear?* 107

MODULE 12: *Your Core Statement*. 111

MODULE 13: *What Value Do You Deliver?*. 119

MODULE 14: *The Role of Storytelling in Marketing*. 123

MODULE 15: *Credibility and Trust: Getting the Client to "Yes"*. 131

MODULE 16: *Offers: How to Give People a Taste of Your Value* 139

MODULE 17: *Rate Packaging*. 145

MODULE 18: *Qualifying People in a Conversation: Knowing Who Is Ready* 155

MODULE 19: *How to Invite a Client Into a Coaching Relationship*. 163

MODULE 20: *Where to Go From "No"?* 169

MODULE 21: *How to Create a Simple Yet Impactful Marketing Plan* 177

MODULE 22: *What Tools Do You Need?*. 187

Table of Contents *(continued)*

MODULE 23: *Building Your Personal Action Plan* 193

MODULE 24: *Leveraging Accountability to Create Success.* 201

MODULE 25: *Marketing Laboratory* 209

MODULE 26: *Learning Debrief* 213

APPENDIX A: *Conscious Marketing Assessment* 217

APPENDIX B: *Conscious Marketing Model* 223

APPENDIX C: *Sample Turnaround Statements for Self-Limiting Beliefs* 227

APPENDIX D: *Student Samples to Inspire New Mental Models* 229

APPENDIX E: *Additional Questions for Guided Vision* 233

APPENDIX F: *Sample Target Market Exercise* 235

APPENDIX G: *Sample List of Solutions* 241

APPENDIX H: *Sample TPS Core Statements.* 243

APPENDIX I: *Student Samples to Inspire Your Storytelling.* 249

APPENDIX J: *Sample Offers.* 253

APPENDIX K: *Sample Rate Packaging* 255

APPENDIX L: *Marketing Plan Template* 257

APPENDIX M: *Find Your Natural Marketing Style.* 261

APPENDIX N: *Top 10 Testimonial Questions by Thomas Leonard* 265

APPENDIX O: *Personal Action Plan* 267

About the Author 269

ACKNOWLEDGMENTS

I want to thank God for testing me rigorously. He has provided me with opportunities to build the internal and external capacity that allows me to be of service to others while enjoying the career of my dreams. I am deeply grateful to have reconnected to my purpose in life and humbled that I found the courage to follow my conviction.

I want to thank my teachers, who inspired me to stretch beyond what I initially thought possible.

I want to thank my students for inspiring me and coaxing me to write this. I want to give a special shout-out to Steph Licata, who practically issued me a mandate (after taking one of my coaching classes at New York University) to document this thinking for others. She inspired me to get it out of my head and onto the page.

I want to thank my book editor, Suzanne Murray, who really got what I was saying and helped midwife this book. She is a talented and conscious entrepreneur.

There is one other very special person—my partner in love and life. I cherish his support and confidence in me.

There are more people I want to thank, but I don't have the space to mention them all. They are friends, confidantes, clients, coaches, and conscious marketers in their own right. I extend my deepest gratitude to you all.

PREFACE

"Nothing happens without personal transformation."

W. Edwards Deming

After a twenty-eight-year career in sales and marketing, the last decade in senior leadership, my career was over in a flash. Part of my golden handshake was a leadership coach to help me through the shock and maze of regrouping.

In the years that I worked for Marsh, the world's largest risk services firm, I coached myself from salesperson to managing director, a coveted slot not held by many, especially women, in my firm. Along the way, I coached hundreds of people to create strategies that would enable them to further their career trajectory in ways that uniquely supported them.

So, in 2004, when my firm laid off 10% of its workforce, me included, little did I know that I was on the verge of reconnecting with my purpose in life. What felt like losing my lifelong career wound up becoming one of my biggest life lessons—and would, in fact, turn me around. Or, more appropriately, turn me *inside out*.

About six weeks into my forced respite, I had an epiphany that was simple yet profound. I was not meant to sell nor lead people who sold and serviced employee-benefits programs. My calling was to be of service to others in their journey of self-actualization—both in their careers and in their personal lives. That's what I had been doing all my life, both inside and outside of my paid work, though I never had a name for it. While my title was "managing director" at Marsh, who I was, really, was a mentor, teacher, advocate—and now that I have a name for it—a leadership coach. If pressed, I described myself as a corporate leader.

Looking back, I can now see how I was afraid to claim my purpose because that would have meant giving up the outward signs of success that I clung to desperately and that others defined me by. I was afraid to find out who I could be without my title, corner office, and track record of corporate success.

This seeming career debacle became an opening for me to live authentically. I would not have had the courage to give up my career at forty-eight to start over. What looked fraught with danger from the outside was actually my portal to freedom, although I couldn't see it at the time. It was time for me to transform and start to live congruently. For me, that meant aligning my "work" with what I valued (learning, relationship, authenticity, and integrity).

Although dubbed a sales and marketing "expert," I didn't know what it meant to market my own brand, be on my own, or live and die by my own creation of revenue or lack thereof. So, becoming an entrepreneur was a huge paradigm shift for me—a total reinvention that would take everything I had to be successful.

Even though I had decades of business experience, going out on my own triggered enormous anxiety. I was nervous about talking about what I did given that the field of coaching is not well understood, even today.

In marketing for my former company, I was able to present myself using a brilliant corporate façade. The firm had over one hundred years of credibility! As a new entrepreneur, I had to figure out how to put my coaching offerings out there in a way that could be heard, and I had to feel natural in doing it. I first needed to shed my limiting belief about marketing myself versus a big company. I had an annoyingly loud voice in my head saying, "You can't compete with the big coaching companies," followed quickly by, "You'll never be ready!" In the beginning, the internal dialogue of fear, doubt, and worry kept me up at night.

My inner critic was successfully chipping away at my confidence, filling me with negative thoughts. Being a coach, I was clear that if I didn't shatter these negative thoughts and consciously create new, empowering ones that I would not be positioned to create what I wanted, which was a new career for myself. I wanted to do great work for people who were ready for and committed to change and I wanted to be compensated commensurately for the results I created. But my fears and insecurities were trying to get the best of me.

I knew I had to kick my negative mental mindsets on their ear, re-examine them, create new ones, and then test those out so that I could pave the path for the success I knew was mine but hadn't materialized just yet. Through trial and error, I figured out how to think anew and what actions to take to proceed with ease, authenticity, and impact.

As you know, my process worked for me. I broke six figures in my third year and my colleagues asked me to help them do the same. This program and workbook reveals the system I created to help my colleagues become conscious marketers and conscious entrepreneurs.

I hope that the material presented here, based on my own struggles and learning, will inspire you to live into your fullest vision for yourself.

HOW TO USE THIS GUIDE

This marketing guide is based on more than three decades of personal business experience, cutting-edge marketing theory, and time spent building two coaching practices from scratch. Within these pages, I share with you my thinking, models, formulas, and tools to use as you see fit.

This guide was created to:

- serve as a learning resource before, during, and after the program
- guide you through the learning process, step by step
- eliminate the need to take copious notes
- give you samples to inspire your thinking
- provide templates to save you time and energy
- reference relevant best practices in the field
- briefly summarize key insights
- outline the classroom exercises you will engage in
- describe the fieldwork, both optional and required, that I suggest.

This marketing guide begins where you might expect—with an introduction of what marketing is, with a special look at the Conscious Marketing system. Next, this guide does something a little bit differently. Instead of jumping right into marketing plans and strategies—tools and tactics—like many books and courses do, this guide will lay the *essential groundwork* for success by exploring your beliefs and mindsets about marketing. Since these beliefs are a fundamental part of whether you will or will not succeed in marketing your practice, we must start there.

Once you have gotten clear on how you are thinking and have begun to make adjustments so your mindsets are maximized, this guide will help you carve out a picture of the kind of practice you would like to create. What is your vision for your practice? Who do you want as clients and what niche are you going to go after?

Only after you have consciously defined and designed the parameters of your unique coaching practice will we begin in this guide (and class) to actively market. Now, with great insight into your special focus, you are ready to construct your marketing message. This portion of the guide will help you determine your value to the client, identify key client-success stories, and more, so that you are able to walk into any room (elevator, or cocktail party!) and talk about your practice with both confidence *and* authenticity.

In the last phase of this guide, we will move into a very practical focus, from setting rates to giving offers. The guide will also arm you with tools for how to qualify leads, invite the high-potential ones to a sample session, and deal when a potential client says "no." Then, we will bring everything together by creating a marketing plan that targets your ideal audience and a personal action plan that tells you when to take which steps. These plans will be based on your dream practice and your strengths in marketing so you can feel excited about marketing, not overwhelmed!

Each module outlined in this guide correlates to a topic we will explore in the classroom and contains a few key elements as follows:

- learning objectives for each module
- concise summary of the topic covered in each module
- brief summary of key insights
- recap of any in-class exercises
- resources you can refer to.

Each module ends with fieldwork to be completed outside of class, with the goal of helping you to continue brainstorming and further refine your ideas, strategies, and plans.[1]

This program takes an action learning approach, and this guide plays an integral role in the learning process. For each module, you will briefly examine the science or theory that informs the module's topic. Then, you will take that abstract knowledge and put it to use by designing practical actions around it. You will then look at the results created by that thinking and action and see what you can learn from it. Then, you will design the *next* step and test those actions out in the real world. For example, you will create messages about what you offer. Then, you will try them on for size by speaking them aloud to a coach buddy. Then, based on your partner's feedback you will refine your messages to be even clearer and more compelling. And so on. It is an iterative process in which you will examine the governing variables (your thinking) and results before designing the next set of actions.

Here are some suggestions, as you get started, to help you get the most out of this workbook and class that you can.

Get Ready to Commit. Do you have the time, energy, and focus to dedicate yourself to learning how to market your coaching practice right

---

1   *Note*: If you have purchased this book outside of my marketing programs or if you are not enrolled in private mentoring sessions with me, think of this book as a self-paced course that you are independently auditing at home. To get the most out of the experience, find a coaching colleague with whom you can do the exercises, share learning, and provide mutual feedback. Also, plan to schedule time on your calendars to explore each module, perhaps one module per week at a time.

now? Are you truly ready to begin? This journey will take personal exploration and growth on your part. Do not start this process until you are ready to do the heavy lifting of thinking and changing. Then, when you are truly ready, make a commitment to yourself. Declare your intention to create new thinking about marketing. You may want to write this intention in a journal or on a sticky note, or say it out loud to a friend. But do declare it.

Find the Right Pacing. Working through this material is akin to working out. As much as I want to work my arms out every day so I can quickly build my biceps, my trainer schedules time off for the muscles to repair and rebuild. Going fast doesn't necessarily produce better results. Like physical training, excavating your profound purpose—and learning how to express it—take time.

As a result, I suggest you read one module of this workbook at a time, in order, and take your time with each. Some modules will take much longer than others. Think about devoting a minimum of one hour to each module.

Accordingly, this workbook is not meant to be read in one fell swoop. You may want to take a fast read though it the first time around just to get oriented, but then, it is best to go back and reread it with the intention of chunking it out over time. You won't get the full value if you read it though once through without working through each exercise. You will get exponentially more from this experience if you deeply engage with the material as you would any university course: read a little, reflect on what you've read, try some of the exercises out, digest the learning and then, write about what your insights, as you feel inspired—a bit at a time. And, if you're up for it, by all means, I encourage you to you to do additional reading and research on the topics that peak your interest.

Dedicate Space and Place to Do This Work. Give some thought to *where* you will do this work. Select what I call a sacred place where you feel safe, and therefore comfortable, to be authentic. No one has to see what you write, so be honest with yourself. You can always tear up or delete what you've written! (Though I don't think you'll want to.)

In addition, give thought to *how* you will document your learning journey. The pages in this manual include space for you to take notes, but if you need more, create a folder or loose-leaf binder where you can add additional notes. Another possibility is to start an electronic or hard-copy journal separate from this manual so you can capture your insights via computer or by hand. Do what works for you. Again, this is your gift to yourself—not some course to pass so you can get your certificate. Do the work, and it will pay off.

Also of note, you will find much practical information in the appendix. It contains templates, assessments, models, and student samples that I have either created, paraphrased, or excerpted to help you push your learning to a deeper level. I have borrowed from many great thinkers, including my students. Please use these as you deem appropriate or create your own.

Redefine Success. This work is an investment in you, reconnecting you to your purpose and bringing that purpose alive. It is special work. This isn't about plowing through a course to get an *A* and be done with it. Truly, if that is the approach you want to take, please put this book down and find a different teacher. I am not for you. My philosophy is that it doesn't matter what the letter grade is; what is important is that you learn and make progress toward your learning objectives, that you leave this class knowing more than when you came in, and that you feel energized to use what you learn to move forward in ways that support your highest development.

This is your life's work. It is about manifesting your purpose so you can make money doing what you love and find a new level of freedom. Don't worry, you may not have it all figured out by Module 2—or Module 10—

for that matter. That's okay. This is a process. It is the work of self-actualization. We go at our own pace. If you try to rush yourself through learning in this class, you may not be able to get as much out of the class as possible. I encourage you to be patient with yourself and the time it takes to absorb all of the material.

And there is plenty of material for us to explore together—all for the good of your coaching business. Shall we begin?

OBJECTIVES

Gain insight into what can be expected from this program

Understand the challenges a coach faces in building a practice

Examine the instructor's observations about what it takes to build a successful coaching practice

Learn how to get the most out of the content and exercises in this class and workbook

MODULE 1: *Ready, Set, Learn!*

About the Program

I believe this is the last marketing course you will ever need. Pretty bold statement. Why do I say that? Because this program addresses the root cause of your marketing dilemmas, not the symptoms. When you address symptoms, you look at what you are doing, how often, and with whom. When you focus on the root cause, you look at your beliefs, motivation, values, and assumptions about marketing, entrepreneurship, and being a coach. When you address symptoms, you can, at best, apply short-term fixes. When you address the root cause, you impact your ability to create a paradigm shift, which in turn catalyzes new behavior, the heart of sustainable change. Treating symptoms is like applying a bandage to a wound—a short-term palliative treatment. Looking at underlying factors can point to the cause of the infection and creates an opportunity to tend to that instead, creating long-term "healing" and even growth. Big difference.

Many marketing courses teach you strategies to try out. That's great—you need them. But strategy is only one third of the equation. Many of you already know that you can use social media, speaking, and blogging to gain client exposure. So the issue you face is not solely "how" to market, meaning which strategies to use. Instead, the challenge is dealing with the reality that you don't actually utilize these strategies or if you do, you may do so sporadically or without taking clear aim with consistent application. So your efforts yield little to no results and you get discouraged.

Let me be bolder still. The root cause of this inconsistent or nonexistent marketing behavior could very well be your deeply seated ideas about marketing—your feelings and beliefs about it. Thoughts like: Marketing is a drag. People may think I am pushy. I am not the sales type. Marketing is an intrusion in people's lives, and I don't want to be thought of that way. I am afraid people may start avoiding me.

Well, let me ask you.

What if marketing was not a dreaded to-do list item?

What if simply showing up naturally could attract enough clients?

What if you felt comfortable talking about what you do for people—as comfortable as you feel talking about the weather?

In this program, you will be exposed to empowering and positive mindsets that can serve as the foundation for the growth of your practice. I invite you to deeply examine these mindsets and, from the menu of choices laid out, play a little game of "Mr. Potato Head," seeing how each feels and, then, building your own mindset for how your marketing could look—one that resonates for you. I am confident that if you are ready and willing to play with alternatives, I can help you shift your paradigm about marketing.

> "Marketing doesn't have to be a 'necessary evil'; instead, it can be a powerful means of communicating about your coaching business in which you feel comfortable, open, and authentic."

Let me begin by reassuring you that you can demonstrate your value to others with dignity, elegance, and integrity. Marketing doesn't have to be a "necessary evil"; instead, it can be a powerful means of communicating about your coaching business in which you feel comfortable, open, and authentic—not cheesy, pushy, or gimmicky. In fact, I see "marketing" simply as a way to communicate the kind of results you create.

If you have an open mind, you will be able to make changes that will result in exponential payoffs, namely, more clients who excite you, are eager to work with you, and pay what you charge without haggling. I have seen this kind of payoff in my own coaching practice as well as with the hundreds of coaches I have taught. That's how I know that this is the last marketing course you'll need.

If you are willing to open your mind and make a commitment to work this program, I will help you create your own authentic mental framework for marketing—one that feels natural and effortless for you, even fun.

The Coach's Challenge

There are a few recurring themes that may lessen or even disable a coach's ability to create financial success. I struggled through many of these and came out the other side. I want to share with you what I noticed and see if you can relate.

Coaches are great at coaching but some do not know enough about how to set up and run a business, which is more than half of what being an entrepreneur is about! Very often, a new coach is building a business for the first time without any experience in how to do so.

Coaches are dealing with stereotypes and fears about marketing that can thwart success at the early stage of business development. Whether it's making a cold phone call or directing someone to a website, coaches may perceive the act of marketing themselves as being "out of character." I believe this is a reaction to some of the unconstructive mental frameworks these individuals have created.

Coaching in and of itself is hard to describe, which makes speaking authentically about it that much more challenging. You can take classes in how to market your coaching services, but they often don't feel genuine. You wind up getting "tools and tips" that make you feel like a salesperson, motivational speaker, or someone hosting an infomercial.

Coaches are not clear on who their ideal audience is—those people who have been waiting for them and who will say yes. In an effort to get business, coaches scatter their seeds widely. They will talk to almost anyone who will listen. This results in low to no impact. This does not make for a positive experience, nor does the coach have the opportunity to truly impact people.

Coaches do not select methods to deliver their message that are natural for them and therefore do not practice them with consistency. Coaches often do shoot-from-the hip marketing, or take the path of least resistance. These actions are based on what they feel like doing, rather than based on an effective strategy thought out point by point and plotted on a calendar over time. Coaches spin their wheels and work hard, not smart. They are left feeling confused as to why they aren't succeeding.

Coaches are isolated, causing them to lose energy and hope. In their struggle to attract clients, fear, doubt, and worry set in. As solopreneurs, there is often insufficient emotional and financial support from colleagues and partners, and coaches eventually make the decision to close down shop.

What It Takes to Build a Successful Coaching Practice

Don't fret, however. These challenges can be overcome! I ask that you consider the following possibilities for creating a successful coaching practice.

If you change your mindset, your outcomes will change for the better. We know that our thinking affects our feelings, which in turn affects our actions—and those actions then determine our results. So, how do *you* think about marketing? If you can change your thoughts about marketing, you can change your future results. If you want to be a successful entrepreneur, you'll need to get past any fears and loathing of marketing.

Learn and practice three basic marketing principles and your business will flourish. Just like

> "If you can change your thoughts about marketing, you can change your future results."

there are three sides to coaching—theory, skill, and presence—there are three sides to marketing. This program will help you develop in all three aspects:

- getting present
- creating compelling messages
- putting them out there strategically.

If you learn how to effectively market—and you can—your business will thrive. With a shift in thinking and a few very simple but powerful practices, you can flourish. Instead of worrying how long your business can be sustained, you will see hope in the warm prospects piling up in your inbox. While word of mouth is great, you will learn to go well beyond this minimal approach, employing instead a rich and targeted marketing strategy.

To this end, this program will help you get clear about:

- knowing who you want to work with
- what their problems are

- what solutions you bring to bear
- what makes you and your offering unique
- what qualifies you to work with these clients
- what you need to do to help your clients move forward with you
- how to attract your prospects' attention, build their desire, and eventually engage with the individuals with whom you most want to work
- how to naturally speak about what you offer.

Your calling is to serve people. Mine is to help you serve people with grace and ease while making money doing what you love. My purpose—and privilege—is to support you in creating a sustainable business by eliminating the shackles that bind you and by creating the mindsets and skill sets that will honor your own purpose.

What It Might Feel Like to Learn in This Program

W.C. Howell outlined a four-step pathway that individuals traditionally go on when learning a new skill. You will likely move through these same four phases (outlined below) as you learn about Conscious Marketing.

1. *Unconscious incompetence* is the "ignorance is bliss" stage. In this stage, you...
   - are unaware of the existence of the skill
   - are unaware that you might have any deficiency in this area
   - might even deny the relevance of the new skill
   - must become aware of your incompetence before you can learn the new skill.

2. *Conscious incompetence* is characterized by anger and frustration. In this stage, you...

- become aware of the existence and relevance of the skill and your deficiency in it
- know what level of skill is required for genuine competence
- make a commitment to learn and practice the skill.

3. *Conscious competence* is characterized by accomplishment and achievement. In this stage, you...
   - can perform the skill without assistance
   - cannot perform the skill unless thinking about it; it is not yet "second nature"
   - should be able to demonstrate the skill to another person but you are still unlikely to be able to teach it well to another
   - should continue to practice to become "unconsciously competent."

4. *Unconscious competence* occurs when learning is intuitive and automatic. In this last stage, you...
   - experience the skills as second nature (e.g., typing, biking, or driving)
   - can perform the skill while doing something else (e.g., crocheting while watching TV)
   - might be able to teach others the skill, but it is so much a part of you it is hard to do so.

Do you remember learning how to drive a car?

Before you got behind the wheel, you might have thought driving was cool and it looked easy. You were in a state of ignorant bliss called unconscious incompetence.

Then, you had your first driving lesson and realized just how much you did not know. This phase, called conscious incompetence, felt awkward.

You may have even gotten angry with yourself or frustrated as you realized that you couldn't drive as well as you would have liked to. This is the point where people tend to give up—*unless* they receive support and encouragement from another.

Then, with practice and encouragement, driving started to become easier, and you reached a point where you could drive—as long as you thought about what you were doing as you were doing it. In other words, you had to "talk yourself" through driving. The internal dialogue might have sounded like this: "Check the mirrors, fasten my seat belt, lock the doors, insert key, foot on brake, hand on stick..." and so on. This phase is called conscious competence. You could drive but you had to pay close attention.

Then, with even more practice, driving finally became second nature. You started the car and drove from place to place while thinking about something else entirely. You didn't have to think about the actual act of driving because you were in a state of unconscious competence, where driving had become part of who you are.

As you sit in this classroom and go through this workbook, you will likely move through the same phases. For example, you may enter this classroom with a big smile on your face, unaware of the challenges before you, a state of ignorance regarding what you don't know yet. By the end of Module 5, you may start to worry and get discouraged as you realize there is much to learn before you can master Conscious Marketing. You will be in a state of being consciously incompetent.

By the last module, you will most likely feel that you can do Conscious Marketing well if you think carefully about your intention and the words you will say—a state of conscious competence. Eventually, you will move to unconscious competence, in which you will have conversations with people you just met about what you do as easily as you would talk about the weather. It is here in this final phase that the skills taught in this course will come naturally to you. In fact, you might even be able to teach them to others. With time, you can enjoy complete ease (conscious competence) in spreading the word about your coaching business.

Preparing to Get the Most Out of This Class

As we prepare to begin our work together, I would like you to clear out a clean "space" for yourself to learn. In addition, I am going to encourage you to put your focus where it will have the most impact—on thinking, vision, and planning. Lastly, I will ask you to commit to certain principles or norms to create a rich learning environment for yourself and your classmates.

Clearing a Space. As coaches, we aim to create a clean space in which our clients can think at the beginning of a coaching session. Our aim is to create an opening for the client to be able to focus his or her attention on the subject at hand. Similarly, we will create a space in this class for you to learn about marketing. To begin this process, please do the following:

- name the concern (worry, fear, distraction) you may be carrying into this class in one sentence
- identify the emotions tied to this concern, using "feeling" words (i.e., nervous, excited, anxious, thrilled, etc.)
- declare your intention to put these feelings aside, just for today, so that you can focus on the learning we are about to embark on.

In this way, you can clear out some of the fears, frustrations, and other emotions that might inhibit you from getting the most out of the learning process. You will be more open and ready to receive the powerful lessons of the Conscious Marketing program.

Where to Focus. There are six levels where you can focus your attention as we move through this material: emotion, problem, detail, planning, vision, and thinking.

I want to encourage you to start practicing the habit of checking in with yourself often as you read, listen, think, and ask and answer questions in this program. Literally pause for a few seconds from time to time and assess where you are thinking from, using the following continuum.

Where Are You Focused?

THINKING/FEELING

VISION

PLANNING

DETAILS

PROBLEM

DRAMA

Let's start at the top.

When you adopt a *thinking* focus, you look at *how* you are thinking about something. This is often referred to as meta-cognition.

In the case of *vision*, you focus on what you want to create—what is possible in the future.

When you adopt a *planning* focus, you aim to create a high-level plan for how to reach your future state.

When you adopt a *detail* focus, you zero in on the various steps and actions you will need to take to get there.

When you adopt a *problem* focus, you look at the challenges, obstacles, and limitations that are perceived or present.

Lastly, when you are in the midst of the negative *emotion or drama* of the situation, you may be focused on any feelings tied to what is occurring or what you may be anticipating in the future.

It is quite natural to spend time focused in each of these areas. The aim, however, is to notice where you are at any given time, decide if it is where you truly want to be, and, if it isn't, aim for a higher level. It's about creating an opportunity to shift your focus if you decide that doing so would yield a better result. This strategy of pausing and checking in gives you a choice. At the choice point, you become accountable to shifting—or not, yielding dramatically different outcomes.

To help clarify these levels of focus, I am going to ask you to think of a gorgeous pre-war limestone building with floor to ceiling windows on Manhattan's Fifth Avenue facing Central Park. The penthouse is the top floor, with a four-exposure wraparound terrace overlooking the park and reservoir. It is the most valuable real estate in terms of price per square foot. Each floor below is a little less valuable in comparable terms.

When learning a new skill, and you will learn many in this program, it is critical to focus your attention where it will yield the most benefit, in this case, the penthouse and top floor of where you choose to focus: thinking and vision. Interestingly enough, about eighty-five percent of most people's thinking occurs in the bottom three levels. Yet, it is at these top three levels that fresh new thinking, and the subsequent motivation we feel as a result, occurs.

Therefore, the three levels we will focus on first are how you are thinking, what kind of vision you are thinking about, and how your thoughts about planning are affecting your marketing

Taking a problem focus (as opposed to focusing on a solution), or staying mired in a negative emotion (the drama in the basement), lessens the likelihood of the type of thinking that would lead to the design of actions that can propel you forward.

For example, you may be feeling nervous about approaching a new prospect to talk about your services. In this situation, I will ask you to pause and get conscious to how you are thinking and feeling about that, and then I will ask if you are willing to put those feelings (nervousness, hesitancy, fear, etc.) aside so that we can explore what you might say if you were not uncomfortable. We do not invalidate your emotion. We

> "When learning a new skill, it is critical to focus your attention where it will yield the most benefit, in this case, thinking and vision."

table it so that we can choose a higher level of thinking—one more likely to result in inspiring action and, ultimately, different results. The more we do so the more we learn how easily we can redirect ourselves and create more action leading to more success.

At any given time throughout this program, I may ask you to pause and ask yourself where you are focusing in that moment. The aim is to help you gain greater awareness of the effect of your focus on your feelings and the results you create. The pause gives you a time-out to take stock of where you are focusing your energy and to allow for a course correction if need be.

So, while you will first identify what's not working and any negative feelings associated with them, you will do so solely to create awareness. Once you have that clarity, you will be invited to take the elevator to a higher floor where the view—and the thinking it catalyzes—is inspirational. Through this process, you will be able to honor your feelings without getting stopped or stuck by them. You will be able to get conscious to your fears and concerns while pushing beyond them in order to develop a plan— and then take action—to grow your business in the way that best supports what you want to create.

"I Am Willing to..."

My aim in this program is to create and sustain a safe and fertile learning environment that enables you to focus your attention without distraction. Setting norms and agreeing to follow them is a prerequisite for this to happen. With this goal in mind, I ask that you read and agree to the following norms by initialing each one. If there are any you do not agree with, it is incumbent upon you to let me know. In that case, I will ask that you propose an alternative you can happily agree to instead. The norms I propose are as follows.

I am willing to:

- Be fully present and give this work my full attention.
- Adopt a mindset of non-judgmental awareness as I listen to others. Whether I agree or disagree is immaterial to listening actively for my own education. I will respect all points of view.
- Try on for size new ideas, behaviors, and voices until I find my own.
- Change and grow. (Be prepared to feel your fears and insecurities. We ultimately need to stare them down to move forward. Your success

will be correlated to your willingness and ability to face the feelings that come up and to work through them.)

- Be responsible for my own learning. It is up to me to extract the value from this learning experience.

- Let go of my preconceived notions about what marketing is and set out to discover it anew.

- Feel consciously incompetent.

- Be called upon several times. I can say "pass" if I so choose.

- Be succinct in what I share and ask.

- Honor time. I will arrive on time, stay until the end, keep to the time allotted for each exercise, and return from breaks in a timely fashion. I understand that the professor will begin whether I show up on time or not. I am responsible for what I miss if I am late.

- Stay on topic.

- Allow the professor to move the agenda forward as she sees fit for the benefit of the class.

- Have fun! I am willing to play and take a light-hearted approach, which means to wonder, discover, and take risks knowing that this is a safe place to do so.

Your willingness to agree to these norms, along with your classmates' equal cooperation, will help us create a rich learning environment that is primed for exploration and growth.

KEY INSIGHTS

- *Marketing doesn't have to be a "necessary evil"; it can be a powerful means of communicating about coaching in which you feel comfortable, open, and authentic.*

- *Getting conscious to how you show up can dramatically shift your results.*

- *There are three sides to marketing: getting present, creating compelling messages, and putting them out there strategically.*

- *The challenges that new coaches face as they start their practices include being skilled at coaching but not at business, being unclear on the ideal audience, and working in isolation.*

- *It will be normal for you to feel like you want to give up as you are learning, and you can even expect to feel awkward, nervous, insecure, and frustrated at times.*

- *The levels of focus that best allow for learning and insight to occur are planning, vision, and thinking.*

Classroom Exercises

Exercise 1-A

Please share the following in thirty seconds:

1. What was your background before stepping into this program?
2. One thing you hope to accomplish as a result of taking this class.

Exercise 1-B

1. Name the concern you are carrying into this class in one sentence.
2. Identify the emotion tied to this concern in one word.
3. Make a declarative statement about putting this concern aside.

Exercise 1-C

1. What additional norms, if any, do you propose?
2. Which do you not agree to? In those cases, what can you happily agree to instead?

Resources

Conscious Marketing Assessment (go to www.conscious-coachinginstitute.com/assess/ or see Appendix A)

Fieldwork

I invite you to take an honest inventory of how you are currently thinking and feeling about marketing as well as your marketing messages, tools, and plans by completing the questions below as well as the Conscious Marketing assessment tool (available in the appendix and online at www.consciouscoachinginstitute. com/assess/). Doing so will help you get clear about your thinking, being, and doing around marketing.

By completing this inventory, you may identify limited thinking, "see" how you're showing up in the world, and be able to evaluate both your blueprint and toolkit for building your coaching practice.

Please rate yourself from 0 to 5 for each statement in the assessment, where *0* indicates no confidence in an area, and *5* indicates a very high level of comfort and strength in the area.

Identify the three areas that you feel you possess the most marketing strength in:

1.

_____

_____

2.

_____

_____

3.

_____

_____

Identify the top three areas in which you want to experience marketing growth:

1.

_____

_____

2.

_____

_____

3.

_____

_____

What patterns, if any, are you seeing?

_____

_____

_____

_____

_____

_____

How have these patterns shaped your results?

_____

_____

_____

_____

_____

_____

OBJECTIVES

*Learn why marketing
is important*

*Define authentic,
conscious marketing*

*Understand a bit about how
successful entrepreneurs think*

MODULE 2: *What Is Conscious Marketing?*

Conscious Marketing Defined

Marketing can be described and defined in a number of ways. Within the Conscious Marketing framework, marketing is defined as authentically and naturally revealing who you are and what you offer, so as to attract and engage the people you most want to work with. It's falling in love again with your contribution and speaking from that place to let people know about what you do for a living and how you can help them. Instead of selling your services, Conscious Marketing is about sharing your life's work. When you begin to think of marketing your coaching practice as simply telling your story, it begins to feel doable, comfortable, and *sincere*.

Think about how you have typically defined marketing up until now and how this definition compares with this idea of telling your story. Does it relieve the pressure to reframe marketing in this way? How might you find renewed energy to market your practice if you had permission to simply *tell your story*? (And, by the way, we will add pieces to that story as this book unfolds, from your core message to client-success stories.)

Why Marketing Is Important

Here is a very real fact. You will not be able to build a sustainable coaching practice if you do not effectively market your business. It does not matter how much you love helping people. It does not matter how many certifications or training hours you have. It will not help a whit that you have your office freshly painted, and your computer, phone, and fax set up—if you do not market your business. People cannot hire you if they don't know about you and what you can do for them!

> "Conscious Marketing is authentically and naturally revealing who you are and what you offer, so as to attract and engage the people you most want to work with."

Here is another very real fact. The top ten percent of individuals with persistence and dedication to their own marketing skills ultimately are the most successful in terms of acquisition of new clients. You see, marketing really does count.

Unfortunately, many coaches do not prosper. The facts are sobering. I don't wish to dwell on them but you need to be aware of them before you put them aside to build what you want instead.

Fasten your seat belt as this is not good news. Don't worry: you are positioned well, being that you are sitting in this class. Nonetheless, here are some important facts I am quoting from Stephen G. Fairley, author of *Getting Started in Personal and Executive Coaching* (pp. 3 & 4).

The facts about new coaches:

- 60% of all second-year coaches have managed to find ten paying clients
- less than 1% of all coaches make more than $50,000 by their second year in practice

- 73% of coaches make less than $10,000 in their first year of practice.

The facts about coaches in general:

- even though coaches charge an average of $160 an hour for their services, 53% of them are making less than $20,000 a year.
- 30% of all coaches are still not able to find ten paying clients
- only 9% of coaches make more than $100,000 a year doing coaching.

I share these facts with you not to depress or demoralize you; I share them because I want to help you understand that coaching is not just a profession but a *business*. No matter how professionally skilled and prepared you are to do the actual work of coaching, you can only succeed financially if you have developed the marketing methods to fill your pipeline with clients!

How Successful Entrepreneurs Think

In my thirty-plus years of sales and marketing experience, I have found that the common denominators of successful marketers are

- *how* they think
- *awareness* of how they think
- a willingness to *refine* how they think to improve their success.

Successful marketers think in a particular way (e.g., positively, confidently, enthusiastically), they are conscious of how their thoughts affect outcomes, and they tweak their thinking when needed to produce more desirable outcomes. These marketers are mindful about what they do: They can tell you what they are doing, how they are doing it, and why. In this process of getting mindful, these marketers define their thinking and refine their thinking. Then, as they see results and receive customer feedback, they learn and adjust their thinking once again. It is an iterative learning process.

The bottom line is that knowing what you're doing and why is fundamental to success.

In Conscious Marketing, you will use that same mindfulness to be successful in your coaching practice. Instead of expecting your business to be successful by default or engaging in random marketing practices, you will consciously select, plan out, and execute your marketing strategies. As you tune into your thoughts around marketing, you will also discover that you are drawn more to some strategies than others. Follow your intuition on this.

As we said earlier, successful entrepreneurs think about *how* they are thinking, which is the premier level of brain real estate. In essence, they are mindful. As a result of being conscious, they are better positioned to succeed.

Remember the model called "Where Are You Focused?" introduced earlier (see Module 1)? Successful people toggle between the higher-level thinking and vision stages in terms of wherever they might be in "a given moment"—and they do so consistently. A given moment could be planning a strategy, putting out a computer fire, creating website verbiage, or dealing with the stress of revenue generation.

As a result of examining how they are thinking about what is occurring, these individuals have a chance to notice whether a discrepancy exists between their intention and the results being created. They ask themselves, "Where am I thinking from right now? In other words, how am I thinking about this?"

For example, you might be so knee-deep in the details that you can't see the forest through the trees. Think of the entrepreneur who spends eight weeks creating a website, goes live, and then realizes that he or she now has to add on another two weeks creating ways to invite people to visit their site. That person was so caught up in one tactical detail of their web-based marketing strategy that they lost sight of the overall aim, which is to meet people live who can then visit the website to cement their credibility by learning more about them.

An important thing to keep in mind is that as an entrepreneur you want to work *on* your business while working *in* your business. You must toggle between vision and details (etc.) to keep things moving forward in a sustainable and profitable manner. Using the strategy of asking yourself *how* you are thinking about *what* you are thinking allows for the kind of pause necessary to make the choice to refocus. This approach can be the difference between staying in the game or stopping because it all feels like too much.

> "As an entrepreneur you want to work *on* your business while working *in* your business."

It's as simple as this. Successful people can hold in mind what they want to be, what they need to do, and what they would like to have (the vision level of brain real estate) all the while that they are operationalizing their strategies. And when they hit a wall—and we all do—they check in with how they are thinking, which is just another way of saying that they ask themselves where they are thinking *from*.

They focus not just on external things like market change but on their inner process. Those who prosper are conscious; they have a thinking map that is logical and repeatable—and the best part is that they feel good about doing it!

KEY INSIGHTS

- *An entrepreneur's way of thinking directly impacts how that person acts—how he or she markets oneself.*

- *If you want to be successful, try on for size the thinking, models, and strategies you will learn in this program.*

Classroom Exercises

Exercise 2-A

What is your definition of marketing?

_____

_____

_____

_____

_____

_____

_____

Resources

Getting Started in Personal and Executive Coaching by
Stephen Fairley

Fieldwork

Create your very own definition of marketing: one that
resonates for you, that can roll off your tongue, and that you
believe to be true for you.

OBJECTIVES

*Learn how the Conscious
Marketing system works*

MODULE 3: *How the Conscious Marketing™ System Works*

Background

There are two essential aspects to the Conscious Marketing system—being and doing. Being refers to the conscious presence you bring into all of your marketing work, and doing is the mode through which you execute your conscious marketing strategy. Let's take a closer look now.

Conscious Marketing™ Unlocked

Being. In most marketing classes, you jump directly into doing. You don't spend time getting conscious on how you think or feel about marketing; you just get cracking on learning and practicing the techniques and the strategies. But as I indicated at the start of this book, marketing techniques themselves aren't novel or mind-blowing. It's the mindset that you bring to your marketing practices that makes all the difference. It is the energy and authenticity—the being, really—that you use to fuel these techniques that makes them so powerful. That is why we will spend so much time in this book focusing on getting comfortable with the idea of marketing yourself and developing techniques that feel reflective of you.

Being true to yourself and claiming your voice is the most important aspect of Conscious Marketing. You want to unearth your authentic voice so that you can speak about what you do in a way that's fully aligned with who you are. Staying connected to your core allows you to speak more openly and from the heart and gives you the freedom to fully step into action. This means falling in love again with what you're offering so you are primed to infuse that energy into all of your communications.

> "A marketing plan is a blueprint for what you will do, with whom, and by when in order to build your client base."

Doing. The doing aspect of Conscious Marketing involves translating your thoughts about the work you do, for whom, and why you do it into tangible action that let's others know about you and your services.

Doing involves crafting a marketing plan as well as crafting the core messages to deliver while executing your marketing plan. A *marketing plan* is a blueprint for what you will do, with whom, and by when in order to build your client base. Within the Conscious Marketing system, that plan is composed of those strategies that most energize and excite you, whether that be blog-writing, speaking, and building strategic alliances, or some other combination.

Regardless of which marketing strategies you ultimately use, the same core message should infuse each one so that you are able to communicate clearly, build credibility, and connect with the right target market. The doing aspect of Conscious Marketing involves crafting these messages.

To help you craft your message, the Conscious Marketing system provides you with plug-and-play formulas into which you can input your unique content and arrive at powerful statements for communicating what you do and the value that you bring. The goal is for you to be able to master a new (marketing) language that allows you to ultimately communicate with ease, clarity, and confidence. In the Conscious Marketing system, you will also discover the role of story-telling to allow for natural conversations that are as comfortable as talking about the weather.

In order to be successful at the "doing" aspect of Conscious Marketing, you will need to stick to your action plan for ongoing success. This means securing strong accountability. One key way of holding yourself accountable is by becoming a member of a mastermind group led by a marketing mentor filled with equally committed, talented, and motivated professionals to stay fresh, inspired, and supportive of each other's pursuit of success.

A mentor helps you develop and refine your marketing plan, shares innovative strategies and insider marketing tips, helps you avoid costly mistakes, and provides accountability for reporting progress made in your plan. With a mentor in place, you will be hooked into

> "It's amazing to see how much faster you grow when led by a marketing mentor and when supported and held accountable by a powerful group of like-minded people who believe in your potential."

accountability for those times when you want to quit. And, let's face it, we all want to quit sometimes! With a high level of accountability, though, you will be able to make smarter decisions and take more action steps, which can get you where you are going faster and easier.

It's amazing to see how much faster you can grow when led by a marketing mentor and when supported and held accountable by a powerful group of like-minded people who believe in your potential. You can do almost anything with that level of energy and support.

Doing therefore starts with finding the conscious entrepreneur within (your being) and bringing it forward in all that you say and do. Once you are truly congruent and aligned with your core, you will show up in such a way that the doing flows easily. Once you begin operating from your authentic core, you will be able to do more than before, with more commitment and focus. You will be able to create opportunities and get better results. You will generate more paying clients, which means you get to make money doing what you love. And you will get to play full out, as an entrepreneur, enjoying the freedom you dreamed about and the financial stability you deserve.

As this book unfolds, we will walk through the Conscious Marketing model step by step. You will discover the various component pieces and their relationship to each other. You will have a plethora of pieces to play with and link together as you see fit, whether you are crafting a flyer, writing verbiage for your website, speaking to a future client, or explaining to your friend what you do for a living.

KEY INSIGHTS

- *To get conscious in your marketing means to get present to how you're thinking, being, and doing to authentically grow your business.*

- *Many entrepreneurs implement marketing activities randomly and get spotty results. By understanding and working this interdependent system of marketing, you'll create consistent and sustainable results.*

- *Your presence, meaning how you show up in the world, starts with your thinking, which influences your being and doing. If you become conscious about who you are, what you do, and what you give others, then your marketing will come from the inside out.*

Classroom Exercises

Let's walk through the several interdependent pieces to the Conscious Marketing model outlined in Appendix B.

Resources

The Conscious Marketing Model (see Appendix B)

Fieldwork

Review the Conscious Marketing model. What are you noticing about each puzzle piece? What are you noticing about how they relate to each other?

OBJECTIVES

*Understand how fear impacts
your ability to learn and grow*

*Learn how the subconscious
mind influences behavior*

*Define what self-limiting beliefs
are and how they impact results*

*Identify the specific beliefs you
hold and learn a strategy to
manage them*

*Learn how to get conscious
and to understand the impact
consciousness creates*

MODULE 4: *Identify the Self-Limiting Mindsets That Hold You Back*

Impact of Fear on Building Your Practice

Many coaches think that they are being proactive and positive in marketing their business because they have created a marketing plan, but unbeknownst to them, they are not really running the show—their subconscious mind is. More than 90% of the time, it's in charge. And much of that subconscious thinking can be negative—self-limiting and fear-based. You may not even be aware you are thinking these toxic thoughts! Yet, they are operating in the background.

There are negative thoughts like: Marketing is annoying to people. They'll avoid me. Or, no one can afford coaching in this economy. Or, what if I fail?

If fear, doubt, and worry are operating in the background of your mind, they're informing your actions (or lack thereof!) without your even realizing it. The result is sporadic marketing or no marketing at all, which translates into a struggle to fill your practice and lack of revenue. Even worse? You don't really understand why you're experiencing lackluster results.

The effect of these negative thoughts is similar to poor nutrition. Your body will run if you feed it junk food, but *how* will it run? Will you have low energy? Will it break down? Will you have a negative body image?

So the question is, when it comes to marketing your business, "What's in your system?" If the answer is negative, fear-based, subconscious thoughts, the next question is, "How do you boost your thinking full of the nutrient-rich thoughts needed to operate optimally?"

Getting Conscious

The first step to a healthy mindset is to get conscious.

This means awakening to your subconscious beliefs around marketing—what you're *really* thinking and feeling and what you maybe didn't even realize was there.

When you identify those subconscious thoughts and feelings about marketing and connect them to how they've compromised your results, you'll finally have the motivation to unhook from those thoughts. You'll be free to disengage from the fear and negative belief systems. This will open a space to create a new mental model for how marketing could look—one that resonates for you and allows you to capture the attention and interest of the people you most want to help.

This is all about waking up to how you show up in the world (i.e., the external impression and messages you convey to others based on your words, tone of voice, body language, etc.) so that you can make *conscious* choices about your actions and the presence you bring into your work and practice. In stages, it's about having a clear understanding of your thinking, being, and doing so you can reach out to potential clients from your most powerful and authentic self, not from your fears or insecurities.

> "By taking a step back and getting present, you can find a new way of thinking that clears the way for all the marketing opportunities to arrive."

By taking a step back and getting present, you can find a new way of thinking that clears the way for all the marketing opportunities to arrive. From this place, marketing can be different, and even fun! In this system of Conscious Marketing, you follow a simple roadmap that gets you from purpose and vision to creating personal action steps for success with confidence and accountability.

Getting conscious offers the opportunity to rid yourself of the anxiety that's typically attached to building a practice. Once you clear the emotional "decks," you can step into the place of presence, where the clarity needed to *choose* a new way of thinking about marketing exists. Creating a new mindset about how you want to communicate the gifts you put forth in the world allows you to capture the attention of the people you most want to attract and engage. Getting conscious creates the opening within—the place where you begin to build your thinking and actions to grow your practice.

Being a conscious marketer means getting to the heart of what it takes to build a client base with less fear, struggle, and effort. It means experiencing the necessary breakthroughs that will release you from your marketing gremlins. To get conscious means that you have shifted your thinking such that a new mindset can emerge. This new mindset dramatically changes your course.

There is no struggle. There is nothing to overcome. There are just your old beliefs about marketing.

Your past doesn't really matter.

Your current circumstances don't really matter.

What people think and say doesn't really matter.

What the voices of fear and doubt say to you do not really matter.

What you believe—now, *that's* what matters!

What you believe becomes true for you. Worried that your prospective clients will think you're too "sales-y" when you speak to them about your services? Your efforts to inform them may just come off sounding weak or cheap. Dwelling on your fear that you are not creative? You may have trouble communicating effectively with your Web designer about what you'd really like to see in your site.

When you pay mind to an idea or feeling, you breathe life into it. So, the aim with Conscious Marketing is to gain increasing awareness of your thoughts and focus so that you can consciously create the marketing results you desire.

Inner Critic vs. Inner Voice

We have two voices within: one is confident and one is scared. One is the inner voice and one is the critic.

What does your inner critic—i.e., fearful voice—say when you think about marketing your coaching practice? I'm sure there are a lot of "what if's" or "if only's." "If only I had more experience," or "what if I don't succeed?" or "if only I had more financial support." Do you see how these thoughts are infused with uncertainty and negativity? Imagine the kind of outcomes you can create with these types of thoughts underpinning your actions. They are likely to be less than ideal.

So, let go of those nagging worries that you've picked up along the way. What matters when it comes to marketing yourself and creating your success is who you are, *in your core*, and what you believe you are capable of in the most positive sense of that term. These are the qualities and types of thoughts that will move you forward in a spirit of creation.

So how do you overcome the "what if's" and "if only's"? Do you ignore your fears or pretend your doubts don't exist? That clearly won't work. The way to handle fear is to become conscious of it—to simply acknowledge it—and move on. We can realize the fear exists, and then refocus our thoughts. The key is to give these thoughts as little energy as possible and give your empowering beliefs this redirected energy instead. This approach will propel you forward, instead of draining you. Each time these fearful thoughts appear, let them go and redirect.

> "The aim with Conscious Marketing is to gain increasing awareness of your thoughts and focus so that you can consciously create the marketing results you desire."

Consciously acknowledge the negative thought and then move on. Be with it and then refocus forward, giving as little energy as possible to it. Every time this negative thought comes up, let it go. Simply noticing your inner critic will help attune you to the fact that you are not the negative thought itself. You are simply "its" observer. This very awareness will help you differentiate yourself from the thought so that it doesn't bring you down with it.

If you are not your negative thoughts—and we are learning that you aren't—then there must be something else inside of you, something deeper, truer, more real. I call that part of you your core. Your *core* is your authentic self—your genuine voice that speaks your essential truth ("I am here to serve." "I have a gift for listening." And so on.) Your core is that pure and confident part of you that came into the world with you at birth—before you rubbed up against an environment that sometimes challenged it, questioned it, or underappreciated it.

When you think from your core—from what you truly know at the deepest level of you to be true—you will feel free, focused, and powerful because you will be coming from a place of authenticity and truth. Imagine you walk into a room full of prospects at a networking event and you are thinking from the realm of your negative thoughts, things like "I'm terrible at talking about what I do for a living" or "People will think I'm being self-promoting if I share what I do." That's very different than entering that same room thinking from your pure and confident core, with thoughts like "I love what I do" and "There are so many interesting people here that I'd love to work with." Can you see how thinking from your core will help you feel more free, focused, and powerful?

This isn't always easy, but it does get easier with practice. In my own experience, there have certainly been times when I am learning skills that push my boundaries, where I have heard the voice of doubt. But then I remind myself to observe the doubt and let it go, and it doesn't take hold of me.

Now, what should be made of all these doubtful and fearful thoughts? Should any of them be taken seriously? Of course, there will always be many reasons why you shouldn't attempt something. Any one of these reasons could stop you in your tracks and prevent you from fulfilling your vision of the future. Over time, though, you can learn to stick with your vision, in spite of the real and seeming challenges and arguments in your way. The doubts and fearful thoughts can be witnessed, but they can then be sent kindly on their way.

What you believe is what will carry you to your future vision and make it your reality—so let's hold onto the positive beliefs and say goodbye to the negative ones. To do so, you don't need to force the negative ones down, back into your subconscious; just observe these negative thoughts and let them float away.

Here's an interesting question: What would you attempt if the inner voice of doubt and criticism didn't matter?? How freeing would that be?

The inner critic says things like, "You'll look desperate if you ask for business. You have got to be kidding me! What makes you think you are qualified to help them? What if you try—and wind up looking like an idiot? What if you ask and someone says no?" And so on.

Truth be told, the inner critic is really good at his or her job, which is to take your worst fears and embed them in your mind. The inner critic attempts to hold you back from playing full out.

Because of the persistent nature of your inner critic, you must acknowledge that it exists and deal with it. Shine light on it. Bring it into conscious awareness. By shining a strong light on it, its power is diffused. After all, your inner critic is not real. It is a script of self-limiting beliefs programmed years ago,

> "By shining a strong light on your inner critic, its power is diffused."

and if you see it clearly for what it is, this perspective disempowers it. Getting aware of the inner critic destroys its power.

The worst thing you can do—that you've probably been doing for years—is try to rationalize your inner critic out of existence, coerce it, or bargain with it. Don't wrestle with it. Simply notice it without agreeing to enmesh. It is a no-win game.

As Oprah Winfrey once said, "You become what you believe; not what you wish for, not what you want, but what you truly believe. Wherever you are in life, look at your beliefs. They put you there."

Oprah did not believe that growing up poor, African American, and female in Mississippi made her less than worthy. Neither did being sexually abused at age nine or delivering a stillborn at age fourteen. "I believed I belonged to someone or something bigger than myself, my family, or even Mississippi. I believed I was God's child. Therefore, I could do anything," she has said.

The best strategy to manage your inner critic is to recognize its existence; then, muster the courage to put the thinking aside for just a few moments so you can get present to what you choose instead.

Harmful Effects of Self-Limiting Beliefs

Limiting beliefs have profoundly negative effects in that they degrade your abilities and program your mind to discard all possibilities for achieving your goals. They lead to procrastination, dampen your hope, shut you down, and have you playing small.

As Eckhart Tolle said,

> The voice in my head tells a story that the body believes in and reacts to. Those reactions are the emotions. The emotions, in turn, feed energy back to the thoughts that created the emotion in the first place. This is the vicious cycle between the unexamined thoughts and emotions, giving rise to emotional thinking and emotional story-making.

Common self-limiting beliefs include the following:

- You are not good enough.
- People will not like you because of your flaws.
- People won't want to hire you.
- You'll be rejected by those whom you ask to work with.
- The economy is bad, so no one is going to spend money on coaching.
- The only way to get rich is to work long, hard hours and sacrifice energy, time, interests, and family.
- Me? Sell? I'll look desperate! Besides, I'm not the sales type.
- What if I ask someone to work with me and they say no? Or avoid me?
- What if I invest money and fail?

- I don't have enough experience.
- I don't think my clients can afford to pay for this.
- How will I ever get from here to there?
- I don't have the resources (the funds, time, help) to make that big dream happen.
- I'm not qualified right now to take on this big dream. I just don't have what it takes yet.
- Once I know how I'm supposed to do this, I'll do it. Until then, I'll just wait to be ready.

And on and on... What does your inner critic say?

It's time to become present to the negative thoughts and beliefs permeating your psyche so that you can observe them, let them go, and lead from your inner core. As you clear the emotional decks, you will find the breathing room needed to awaken the authentic you that is ready and able to connect to the clients that you most want to work with.

KEY INSIGHTS

- *Our subconscious minds are in charge much of the time—they drive our behavior.*

- *A self-limiting belief is a negative, persistent thought pattern (also known as an inner critic or gremlin) that curtails a person's ability to create success.*

- *Self-limiting thoughts shape our actions, and therefore we need to get conscious to them in order to then turn them around.*

- *The best strategy for dealing with negative thoughts is to simply notice them, put them aside, and create new empowering thinking instead.*

Classroom Exercises

Exercise 4-A

1. What does your inner critic say? Write out your top three self-limiting beliefs.

> Sample: I'm not the sales type and I hate to be perceived as needing someone's money. I find it embarrassing and uncomfortable.

a.

_____

_____

_____

b.

_____

_____

_____

c.

_____

_____

_____

2. Write out the turnaround statement for each, framed in a positive way.

> Sample: I choose to be natural and unassuming when sharing what it is that I create for others.

a.

_____

_____

_____

b.

_____

_____

_____

c.

_____

_____

_____

Resources

Student Sample Turnaround Statements for Self-Limiting Beliefs (see Appendix C)

Student Samples to Inspire New Mental Models (see Appendix D)

OBJECTIVES

Understand the nature of mental models and how they shape your actions

Get clear about your current mindsets about marketing

Construct new empowering mental mindsets to ensure your success

MODULE 5: *Creating New Mindsets*

What Is a Mental Model?

We have talked lots so far about how fearful thoughts and a negative mindset can affect your marketing performance. Now, let's look at the mental models at the heart of these mindsets. A *mental model* is a belief structure about how things work.

Let me share with you what Peter Senge has to say about mental models. Senge is Director of the Systems Thinking and Organizational Learning Program at MIT's Sloan School of Management. The following summary is from Chapter 10 of his book, *The Fifth Discipline: The Art and Practice of the Learning Organization.*

> [Mental models are] deeply ingrained assumptions, generalizations, or even pictures or images that influence how we understand the world and how we take action. The discipline of working with mental models starts with turning the mirror inward; learning to unearth our internal pictures of the world, to bring them to the surface and hold them rigorously to scrutiny.

Mental models shape how we act. Therefore, the challenge with having a mental model of anything lies not in whether that model is right or wrong (by definition, all models are wrong as they are all simplifications). The problem is that they often exist below our level of awareness and yet they drive our behaviors—often, in ways that do not serve us! Now, let's explore the link between the mental models you are using and your marketing results.

Mental Models Drive Action and Outcomes

Our mental model of marketing—our way of looking at marketing—is just *one* way of looking at the marketing process. The question to ask then is not "Is my particular mental model *correct*?" but instead "Does my mental model serve *my goal*?"

If you are not ready to hear anything else in this class, please hear this: Your mental models shape how you act. If you want different results, you need to change how you look at and think about marketing.

I am reminded of a client who had a successful shamanic healing and coaching practice who dreamed of taking her business global. Yet, there were these nagging, negative thoughts holding her back, things like, "How dare I ask for something like that? I should be grateful for what I have and not want even more. Maybe going global isn't possible for me." But that was just her inner critic speaking.

> "A mental model is a belief structure about how things work."

We stayed with these negative thoughts and her fears long enough to help her work through them. She managed to shift her mental model so that instead of being built on thoughts like, "I have no right to ask for that...who do I think I am?" it was built on thoughts like, "I want to help more people wherever they may be." These thoughts naturally set her up to start marketing with a different mindset. She no longer felt tied.

For example, she began marketing her services in a way that people who were out of the country could partake virtually, through teleclasses. She also offered remote healing sessions. Within months, she was global! She now partakes in retreats outside the United States. This year, she was in Egypt.

My client's successful ability to market globally stemmed from a clear shift in mental models—from one based on fear of playing full out to one based on the idea of "This is what I choose to create in the world." As Dr. Wayne Dyer said so eloquently, "If you change the way you look at things, the things you look at change."

So, we have these beliefs powering our action engine and yet we are not consciously aware of what some of the beliefs are. It's time to get conscious.

What Is Your Mental Model of Marketing?

It is easy to have negative feelings and thoughts about sales and marketing. Let's face it. There is a preponderance of negative messages in the market-place that have affected us since we were very young.

Case in point: I remember being a young girl wanting one of those famous hamburgers I saw on the television commercials. My mother made rubbery things that were fried in a pan and that dripped with grease that soaked through boring white bread. After months of my asking, she finally gave in and took my brother and me to the fast food restaurant to get our treat. When I opened the wrapping and saw this wimpy, beige sliver of meat, I was incredulous and disappointed. I was convinced that my mother ordered the wrong burger! She assured me she didn't. It just couldn't be! But, alas, it was.

In that early moment, what I learned was that marketing was tantamount to lying and that it happens every day. I have been carrying that mental model, and others equally as negative, with me a long time. When I first started my coaching practice, those images and feelings were tacit. I hadn't thought back to that incident; I just saw my lack of ease in speaking about what I could create for clients.

Once I identified my disempowering mental models, I was able to redirect my thinking to the kind that now propels me and creates success for me every day.

What are the mental models you are carrying? What might you be holding in your mind that you may not even be consciously aware of?

Have you ever experienced the following? I sure have.

- a steak house selling the sizzle, not the steak
- a real estate bait and switch
- getting caught in the fine print on a contract
- ordering a catalog item only to find out it looks different in person
- airbrushed photographs
- buying a car only to find out it is a lemon
- price-gorging on an item when there is a disaster or emergency

Don't underestimate how these kinds of events have informed your feelings about marketing yourself today. As Carl Jung so aptly said, "Until you make the unconscious conscious it will direct your life."

It is true. We know that we become what we think about. We also attract what we think about. It is the law of attraction. Thoughts emit a frequency similar to a television where each channel emits a different frequency. If we want different results (in marketing or life), we must look at, and then change, the frequency (nature) of the thoughts we are thinking.

Creating new thinking is actually quite simple. You are doing it all the time (without even trying). You are creating new thinking maps right now as you read this passage!

An inspiring story of how we can change our thinking is evident in the story told by Viktor Frankl, in *Man's Search for Meaning*. During his imprisonment in a Nazi war camp, Frankl was fed, by his captors, a bowl of filthy water with a fish head floating in it. He talks about training himself to see the beauty in this meal rather than the horror of it. As Frankl noted, "Everything can be taken from a man but one thing: the last of the human freedoms—to choose one's attitude in any given set of circumstances, to choose one's own way."

Fortunately, when it comes to marketing, you will not have such dire circumstances but you may find yourself trying on new behaviors that at first feel quite uncomfortable. If you

> **"If we want different results (in marketing or life), we must look at, and then change, the nature of the thoughts we are thinking."**

choose to apply a Conscious Marketing approach, you will pay mind to the negative thoughts that may arise in order to let them go and shift toward the positive. In the process, you will arm yourself with a powerful tool for attracting and retaining your ideal clients.

Shifting Your Thinking and Finding Your Truth

Our minds move at lightning speed. Ironically, this *slows* our learning, because we immediately "leap" to conclusions so quickly that we often do not test them in the real world—and end up acting on false premises that lead to undesirable outcomes. These are referred to as "leaps of abstraction" because they are not based on hard evidence.

How do you successfully handle a leap of abstraction when it occurs? First, you must notice it; let the light bulb go on (e.g., "I just made an assumption—an unhelpful leap"). Once you notice it, turn that light onto identifying what conclusion you are drawing (e.g., "People will see my tweets as spam" or "People will throw my marketing postcard in the trash without reading it"). Next, ask yourself what belief of yours regarding the way marketing, business, and people work is fueling you to draw that conclusion or make that leap (e.g., "All tweets from professionals and organizations will be seen as spam. I will be unable to post messages of value and interest to my Twitter followers.") In other words, ask yourself what this conclusion is based *on*.

Then, are you willing to consider that the conclusion you have reached is inaccurate? If the answer is no, there's no point in proceeding. You have to be genuinely curious and willing to adjust your mental model for change to occur. You have to be willing to expose the limitations in your own thinking. You have to be willing to be wrong.

Next, to market yourself without sacrificing your integrity, you need to find the place within where you speak the truth of what you can do, neither underselling nor overselling yourself and your services. Without bragging or playing small, you need to be able to communicate what is so.

To do this means that you have to replace playing small ("I'm not worthy") and bragging ("I am the world's best coach") with authentic and congruent thoughts ("I have real value to offer"). For example...

> *Playing small:* I'm not sure what my clients want or need.
> *Bragging:* I know what my clients need better than they do.
> *Authentic:* I work to understand the needs and concerns of my clients.

> *Playing small:* I'm not sure that my service will make a difference.
> *Bragging:* My services are the answer to everyone's problems.
> *Authentic:* I know I have valuable services that can help.

Playing small: I can't think of that many stories about my clients' success.

Bragging: I've performed literal miracles for my clients.

Authentic: I have stories and examples that prove my value.

Playing small: When I get my graduate certificate in coaching, I'll feel more competent.

Bragging: I'm the best coach ever. Period.

Authentic: I know what I'm doing. I'm competent and professional.

Playing small: I try and try my best, but I'm not sure that's enough.

Bragging: Clients never appreciate what you do, no matter how hard you try.

Authentic: I can be counted on to always serve my clients' best interests.

Playing small: People really don't want to hear about my services.

Bragging: If you can't dazzle them with brilliance, baffle them with bull.

Authentic: I need to educate my prospective clients about what I do.

Playing small: I'll do absolutely anything my clients ask of me.

Bragging: I'll go the extra mile if I get paid for my time.

Authentic: I first put my attention on the needs of my clients.

Playing small: I don't want to appear pushy or sales-y.

Bragging: All my clients buy my biggest package whether they need it or not.

Authentic: I make recommendations that are based on what I can deliver.

Playing small: I can't charge that much for my services because I am not an MCC.

Bragging: I charge whatever the market can bear and then some.

Authentic: I charge a fair price for my services and give value in return.

Playing small: I'm grateful my clients use my services at all.

Bragging: My clients don't have their act together.

Authentic: The relationship with my clients is one of mutual respect.

What are the messages and beliefs that have you playing small? How might you reframe those thoughts to support your moving forward in a powerful way?

KEY INSIGHTS

- *Our thoughts (mental models) shape our actions.*

- *We are not stuck with our current mental models. It is possible to create new ones.*

- *The key to identifying our mental models is being aware of the gap between our thoughts and actions.*

- *The opposite of playing small is not being grandiose. It is finding your quiet and confident truth.*

Classroom Exercises

Exercise 5-A

Think of a time when you connected with someone and really got something across in a natural, comfortable way—in a way that really inspired them.

1. When was it? How did you feel at the time?

_____

_____

2. What was different in your mind as compared to a time when you might have felt nervous or awkward?

_____

_____

3. What was your mental movie before starting the interaction?

_____

_____

 Exercise 5-B

Write out the mental model of marketing that you wish you had, but don't right now. For example, you could answer this question: "To feel great about marketing and be successful beyond my wildest dreams, my view of marketing would have to look like this..."

_____

_____

_____

_____

_____

_____

_____

_____

_____

_____

_____

_____

_____

_____

_____

_____

_____

_____

Resources

The Fifth Discipline: The Art and Practice of the Learning Organization by Peter Senge

Student Samples to Inspire New Mental Models (see Appendix D)

Fieldwork

Write out what you want to create in the present tense and framed in the positive, pretending that you already have it for each of the topics below. (Tip: You can use the phrase "I choose" to frame it in the present tense. For example, you can go from "I want to stop struggling to attract clients" to "I want to attract new clients more easily" to "I choose to have a full practice.")

Clients

_____

_____

Money

_____

_____

Prospecting

_____

_____

My Services

_____

_____

Rejection

_____

_____

OBJECTIVES

*Get clear about your vision of
yourself as a future coach*

*Envision the type of practice you
choose to create*

MODULE 6: *Connecting to Your Vision*

A Guided Imagery Experience

In order to get clear about your vision for yourself as a future coach, I would like to introduce you to a guided imagery exercise. (If by chance you are reading this at home, and not in my classroom, I ask you to put some time on your schedule, right now or sometime this week, and conduct the following exercise.) By engaging in this experience, you are likely to see more clearly what it is that you want to create for yourself and your practice.

This guided meditation was written by Edward J. Twomey, based on a guided imagery activity entitled, "Window," by Larry Moen, in *Guided Imagery: Volume One*, United States Publishing, 1992, and is reprinted here with permission. You can work through this exercise as you read it, or better yet, make a recording of it on your smart phone or digital recorder and, then, find a quiet place where you can close your eyes and listen to what you recorded.

The Window in the Forest: A Guided Journey for Career Development

"Close your eyes and take a deep breath. Exhale slowly, letting go of all of your muscles from your scalp to your toes. Relax completely. Inhale again.

Slowly exhale, releasing any remaining tension in your body.

As you continue to breathe, deeply and steadily, let your mind relax and drift gently until you find yourself standing on a pathway—the kind of clear, cool, dirt pathway you often find walking in a New England woods in early summer. The pathway feels firm and smooth beneath your feet. You begin to move forward at a relaxed pace. You are feeling confident and easy, glad to be here on this pleasant, warm summer day.

> "As you continue to breathe, deeply and steadily, let your mind relax and drift gently until you find yourself standing on a pathway."

A lush green forest spreads out on either side of the path. No branches or brush are in your way as you move along the pathway. No rocks or logs are at your feet. So the going is smooth and easy, and the pace remains relaxed as you walk along through the forest. Warm dapples of sunlight make their way through the trees, and in little clearings on either side of the path you see patches of daisies, and bouquets of black-eyed Susan's, and little nosegays of wild violets scattered among the taller flowers. Here and there, on either side of the pathway, you see soft pink and crimson wild roses on deep green bushes. You inhale the sweet smell of the roses, and their scent stays with you.

As you look ahead along the pathway, you see rays of the sun coming through the trees. There is still some morning dew on the leaves of the trees, and the sunrays glisten and sparkle when they meet the dewdrops.

You continue to move forward along the path. As you look ahead, you see a small clearing in the forest, and in the clearing, a door appears, just a short distance ahead of you. It is freestanding, connected to nothing you can see, except the archway of wild roses that you would have to pass under to get to the door.

As you draw near the door, and pass under the archway, you notice a large window inset in the door. You arrive in front of the door and peer through the large window. You stand and look, aware of your confidence and inner strength. And as you continue to look through the window, you realize that you are looking at a future scene you have created for yourself. You can see yourself appear in this scene. You look very much as you do now—on those days when you know you are looking your very best. So you know it is not that far ahead in your life; perhaps two to five years from now.

And as you watch yourself, you realize that you are looking happy and content. And it comes to you that the you that you are watching is moving within a setting where you are doing your work, pursuing the career vision and dreams you imagined for yourself back in the (insert season) in the year (insert year).

What is this place in which you see yourself? Where are you? What is your work like? What is its purpose? Are there customers or clients? Are there products or creations? Are there services or skills produced for others' needs or benefits?

What is the physical space like in which you do this work? Are you in a building? Outdoors? A city? A town? The countryside?

Do you have a workspace? What does it look like? What does it feel like? Are there others in this work setting? Who are they? What are they like? What is your relationship to them? How do you interact with them? How do you do your work with them?

Is there evidence of your core values in this scene? How do the things you remember being dearly important to you in (insert year) find their way into this scene you are watching?

You are able to see how wonderfully content you appear in this scene as you move about. What is it about the way your career has blossomed for you that brings you this feeling?

As you continue to look through the window, the scene blurs ever so slightly, and starts to change. But you are not frightened. You know what is occurring: You are watching the setting shift to where you live in this not-so-distant future.

What is that space like? What does it feel like to be there?

Are you in this space with others? Who are they? What is it like to be with them?

What is your most private space in this place like? How have you made it yours?

Are there life interests and activities you love to do going on here? What are they? And how do they fit into the parts of your life? As you observe yourself in this scene, you again notice how content you appear—how satisfied and passionate you are about your life and work.

> "What is this place in which you see yourself? Where are you? What is your work like? What is its purpose?"

It is time to go now. Turn away from the door. Pass under the archway of roses again, and onto the pathway. The day is still as it was—warm sun, cool shade, fragrant wildflowers. You head back along the path that led you here. The ground is still firm beneath your feet. As you walk, you hear the slight rustle of the trees. You become aware of the soft sound of your footsteps and of the sweet serenades of songbirds.

You are back in this room now. You are feeling more awake, more alert, more aware of your breathing. You feel your body again, but it is relaxed. At the same time, you are energized, ready to remember and to hold onto all that you saw and felt on this journey.

Breathe deeply, letting your breath revitalize your body. Slowly curl and release your fingers and toes. Gently stretch every muscle, awakening each one individually.

Take a deep, deep breath, and exhale. And when you are ready, open your eyes."

Take a moment to fully refresh and, then, when you are ready, start answering the questions in Exercise 3-A below. You can answer the questions in a stream of consciousness. Just write what comes up. No need to edit. We will come back to your answers as fieldwork, when you can take an hour or more to polish them up.

KEY INSIGHTS

- *You can reconnect to your vision for yourself as a coach and learn about what it is you want to create for yourself by tapping into guided meditation.*

- *Give yourself time and space to imagine the ideal coaching and life situation for you. It is possible to create it—once you have a picture in your mind!*

Classroom Exercises

Exercise 6-A

Answer the following questions in a stream of consciousness. Just write what comes up. No need to edit just now. We will come back to your answers as fieldwork, when you can take an hour or more to polish it up.

1. What specialized knowledge do you have to bring to bear for clients' benefit?

_____
_____
_____

2. What is the value you provide in the role you envision for yourself?

_____
_____
_____

3. Which segment of the population are you working with? Describe them.

_____
_____
_____

4. What problems do the client groups you are working with have?

_____
_____
_____

5. How do you imagine your paths crossing with them?

_____
_____
_____

6. What are the benefits to others of providing this service?

_____

_____

_____

7. How do you know you provide the value and benefits that you do?

_____

_____

_____

8. What qualities do you see that you and your work embody?

_____

_____

_____

9. What are you getting out of your work?

_____

_____

_____

Resources

Additional Questions for Guided Vision (see Appendix E)

Fieldwork

Finish fleshing out the answers to the questions (see previous Classroom Exercise) asked in response to the guided imagery exercise outlined in this module. Then, look at everything on your page. What would excite you even more?! (If you need additional space, write your answers below.)

1. What specialized knowledge do you have to bring to bear?

_____

_____

2. What is the value you provide in the role you envision for yourself?

_____

_____

3. Who are you working with? Describe them.

_____

_____

4. What problems do the client groups you are working with have?

_____

_____

5. How do you imagine your paths crossing with them?

_____

6. What are the benefits to others of providing this service?

_____

_____

7. How do you know you provide the value and benefits that you do?

_____

_____

8. What qualities do you see that you and your work embody?

_____

_____

9. What are you getting out of it?

_____

_____

OBJECTIVES

Learn what a target market is

Identify your ideal client profile

Define the characteristics that compose your target market

MODULE 7: *Identifying Your Favorite People to Work With*

Target Market Explored

A *target market* is a group of people you choose to work with.

Without a clear and comprehensive picture of who you want to work with, there's not much point in going further. The purpose of your services is to solve problems. If you don't know who your clients are, inside and out, you will not be able to identify them, nor their problems.

When you get crystal clear on who your target market is and when everything you say and do expresses that clarity, the audience you want to support will know you are committed to serving them. You may very well be the answer to their prayers, if you can define exactly what your target market wants. Truly knowing who your ideal clients are positions you to accomplish even greater results and to experience incredible fulfillment.

What Is Your Purpose?

It's my strong belief that every human being is on Earth for a reason. You too were created for a specific purpose, and you therefore have a specific assignment—a problem that you have been uniquely sent here to solve.

Are you a solution to everyone's problem? No. Instead, you must find which group of people you have been sent to serve and focus on that segment of the human population. You must say yes to this unique audience so that you can give your best to them and avoid diluting your focus and attention.

When you engage in Conscious Marketing, you end up being able to focus your gifts in a niche market that has a problem you can solve in a way that only you can. There are people in the world who can only hear the message you have, from you. They are waiting.

Who Have You Done Your Best Work for?

To get you started on defining your ideal target market, I want you to think of three clients for whom you have done your best work. What's common among them? Considering your success with these three clients, what is it that you've been designed to do? Who have you been designed to do it with? And what outcomes have you been designed to create with this particular group of people?

The answers are already within you—you do not need to create them. Under the right conditions, these answers will become conscious, and together they will be a game changer.

> "Knowing who your ideal clients are positions you to accomplish even greater results and to experience fulfillment."

We all have a purpose, a thing we were designed to do, but sometimes we are unclear about that purpose. Until we get clear, our business will not be as powerful as it can be.

Classroom Exercises

Exercise 7-A

Who do you see yourself providing value to?

_____

_____

Who would benefit from your unique combination of experience, passion, and talent?

_____

_____

What type of people do you love being around?

_____

_____

Who are the people who inspire and energize you?

_____

_____

Who do you have the most fun and energy around?

_____

_____

Make a long list of the characteristics that these people have.

_____

_____

When do you feel most passionate?

_____

_____

What would you do even if no one were paying you?

_____

_____

Exercise 7-B

Name three clients for whom you have done your best work.

_____

_____

What's common among them?

_____

_____

What is it you've been designed to do?

_____

_____

Who have you been designed to do it with?

_____

_____

And what outcomes have you been designed to create with those people?

_____

_____

 *Exercise 7-C*

My top three target markets:

1.

2.

3.

KEY INSIGHTS

- *A target market is a group of people you choose to work with.*

- *If you don't know your target market intimately, you will not be able to identify what they want and need.*

- *Another benefit of knowing your target well is that it ensures better results for them and more fulfillment for them.*

- *Avoiding less-than-ideal clients is a smart business decision.*

Resources

Sample Target Market Exercise (see Appendix F)

Fieldwork

1.   Know your ideal client profile, inside and out. Create a list of his/her characteristics:

Age range:

Gender:

Level of education:

Geographic location:

Income level:

Life stage:

Ethnic group:

Profession:

Industry:

Position:

Personal interests:

2. Additional questions to think about:

When do they buy what you're selling?

How do they buy your services?

What do they perceive they are buying?

Why should they buy from you?

How do they talk about their challenges or issues?

What specific words or phrases are they likely to use when describing their problem?

What other types of professional services do they buy?

Who do they have regular contact with?

Who are they likely to turn to when making a difficult decision?

What kinds of people or businesses do they trust?

Preferred style of communication (email, phone, or in person?)

How do they buy your kinds of service?

What do they perceive they are buying?

Why should they buy from you?

OBJECTIVES

Learn what a niche is and explore types of niches

Select your niche(s)

Examine the challenge of staying true to your niche

MODULE 8: *Determining Your Niche*

What Is a Niche?

When you choose to focus your marketing effort on a specific segment of the population that is most likely to value your services, it's called choosing a niche.

A niche allows you to establish a unique identity that favorably sets you apart. It conveys what you stand for.

A *niche market* is a small, well-defined segment of a larger market, with common characteristics and needs. Some example niche market segments include CEOs, leaders, female entrepreneurs, parents, baby boomers, teens, the lesbian-gay-bisexual-transgender (LGBT) community, singles, Christians, couples, and small businesses.

A *niche service* is created to meet the needs of a niche market (for example, my OneSource mentoring program was created for coaches who seek International Coach Federation credentialing, a niche market segment).

A niche business is built entirely to serve a niche market (for example, my Conscious Coaching Institute was built to address the needs of the above niche market by providing professional development and practice development).

Why Carve Out a Niche?

While selecting a niche (or niches) is not a requirement, especially when just starting out, choosing a focus allows you to target your energy more effectively and also helps potential clients to find you more easily as you will be known for something.

The benefits of catering to a niche market include greater gains in happiness, satisfaction, and revenue over the long-term. This is because you get to

- enjoy the clarity of knowing whom you want to market to, which makes your marketing tasks easier and more effective (increased revenues)

- work with the group of individuals that most interests you (increased satisfaction)

- become expert at a specialized skill set, which will make you better at what you do and give you an edge over your competitors (increased revenues and satisfaction).

In addition, you will stand out from the crowd and "speak" directly to those who really need your services. You will also make it easier for other professionals to refer clients to you because they will know exactly what you do and which clients are the right match for you.

Once you have identified your niche, it's time to let others know about it. Your goal is to

> "Choosing a focus allows you to target your energy more effectively and also helps potential clients to find you more easily as you will be known for something."

communicate your niche clearly and consistently so that potential clients can easily identify who you are and what you do. Through your consciously crafted cards, brochures, e-mail signature blocks, website, stationery, advertising, and more, potential clients should be able to recognize what your niche is.

Lastly, once you have your niche, you will need to resist the urge to dilute it and be all things to all people. Having a marketing campaign clearly targeted to that niche will help attract the right crowd, but when stray opportunities to work with those outside of your niche present themselves, think carefully about taking on that work. My recommendation is to stay true to your identified focus, having trust in your ability to attract those with whom you really want to work.

> "Stay true to your identified focus, having trust in your ability to attract those with whom you really want to work."

Only when you leave a space open for these clients can they find their way into your practice.

I would make one exception to this recommendation to hold tight to your niche. If you are just starting out in coaching and would like to log hours in order to hone your skills, it may make sense to see a variety of client types in the beginning. As you log hours and sharpen your skills, you will also be able to test out the markets that you most resonate with. Once you have 100 hours under your belt, you will feel better positioned to know who you really want to work with and where you do your best work. You can then identify your niche and begin marketing to these individuals.

The benefits of focusing your energy on the specific group that fully appreciates your value—and is prepared to pay for it—will result in greater gains in happiness, satisfaction, and revenue over the long-term.

KEY INSIGHTS

- *To be effective, consider selecting a niche.*

- *Catering to a niche will help you become expert at a certain skill set, work with your ideal audience, and stand out from the crowd.*

- *Staying true to your niche will yield greater benefits to you and those you serve.*

Classroom Exercises

Let's think about those segments of the population who would value most what you offer. Then, write about what comes up for you.

My niches:

_____

_____

_____

My niche market:

_____

_____

_____

My niche service:

_____

_____

_____

My niche business:

_____

_____

_____

What is the benefit to you of working with this portion of the population?

_____

_____

_____

Fieldwork

Set aside thirty minutes to think more about your niche in the hopes of getting even clearer. Keep a pen and paper by your side—or this workbook—and jot down notes on your different ideas. You can build on the brainstorming work you started in class or come up with additional ideas.

OBJECTIVES

*Understand what a brand is and
get clear about yours*

*Discover why creating and main-
taining your brand is important*

Learn how to express your brand

*Understand what makes you
unique as a coach*

*Be able to speak about who you
are and what you deliver with
clarity and ease*

MODULE 9: *Communicating Your Brand*

Background

In order for someone to identify with you and say yes to your services, that person has to be clear about who you are and what you deliver. He or she needs to know what problems you solve and what solutions you help facilitate—that is, what you do and how you do it unique to you. All of this together represents your brand. Being able to express and exude this uniqueness is your responsibility as a conscious marketer. Then, whether a client identifies with you is up to them.

What Is a Brand?

A *brand* is a unique promise of value. Defining your brand is about unearthing who you are and what makes you exceptional so that you can express that gift in clear, inviting terms.

Who are you as a coach? What do you stand for? What is your passion? What is your strength? What is your gift to share with the world? What gets you out of bed in the morning?

The goal of a brand is to:

- develop a clear, relevant, and memorable message
- set you apart
- help people remember and value you
- convey what you stand for.

Your brand must be differentiated and compelling; it should express who you are authentically and build emotional connections. Buying is emotional and branding is meant to help you build those emotional connections.

If you don't stand out, you are relegated to being a commodity—and when someone hires you it's only a matter of price. Compare the difference: Coffee is a commodity, but Starbucks is a brand. If I just want coffee, I seek to pay the least for the best (I make a decision on price). If I want to go chill in a big chair and take in the vibe, I go to Starbucks and am willing to pay four dollars a cup (I make a decision based on brand).

Likewise, if you are just "a coach," you're a commodity. If you're a brand, you will stand out. Think of these people: Madonna, Lady Gaga, Kim Kardashian. Each has a brand. They each exude that brand in spades.

> "Defining your brand is about unearthing who you are and what makes you exceptional so that you can express that gift in clear, inviting terms."

Branding is not about pleasing everyone nor is it about being all things to all people. In fact, a strong brand will repel as much as it will attract. If you Google "I love Gaga" and "I hate Gaga," you will see two very strong camps. Either you love or hate her. Either you love or hate Starbucks. As Bill Cosby once said, "I can't tell you the key to success but I can tell you what it is not: Trying to please everybody."

If you have a brand, some people will be attracted to it; others will believe that it's not right for them. But with a brand, you will be known for something, and the people who want what you offer will hear about you and be interested.

As noted in *The Heart of Marketing*, "Identification happens when your potential customer sees themselves in you. They recognize their experience in what you are presenting. And in their recognition they see you as an extension of themselves. That's how every sale is made, through the internal identification in which two parties see themselves in one another."

So, in reality, none of us has true "competitors." Yes, there are other coaches in your niche, but each person is unique in terms of background, training, experience, and style. You are not them. They are not you. This is why your ability to know and express your brand is important. You are not a commodity.

How do you want people to feel when they meet you and read your messages? What image do you want to project? What tone do you want to set? All of these answers combine together to help you create and define your brand.

Benefits of Knowing Your Brand

There are benefits to you for creating and expressing your brand. They are:

- greater visibility in the marketplace (people will recognize your service as an attractive and viable option)
- stronger presence (your brand will exude a sense of reliability and permanence)
- differentiation (people know why to hire *you* rather than someone else).

In addition, awareness of yourself increases when you know your brand because the process itself of defining and creating your brand force you to become clear on who you are and what your purpose is. In turn, the clarity required to *communicate* your brand lends itself to full expression of your values, and that is powerful and attractive to those it speaks to.

William Arruda has a model for thinking about one's brand. He says we need to do three things:

- extract it – unearth your unique promise of value
- express it – communicate your brand to your target market
- exude it – align your brand environment so it is congruent.

The key to branding is to communicate your brand clearly and consistently. Let everyone know who you are and what you do. You will have a chance to practice doing this—what I call telling your story—in the fieldwork for this module.

Know Your Story

The foundation of your brand begins with your story—your background, why you coach, your strengths and unique characteristics, your commitment to your others and more. By building your story on paper and then simply allowing your brand to emerge from that story, your marketing flows from a very real place. You won't be promising more than you can deliver or be giving false impressions (remember the steakhouse sizzle and fast-food hamburgers that sorely disappoint?). You'll be offering an authentic you!

My Story

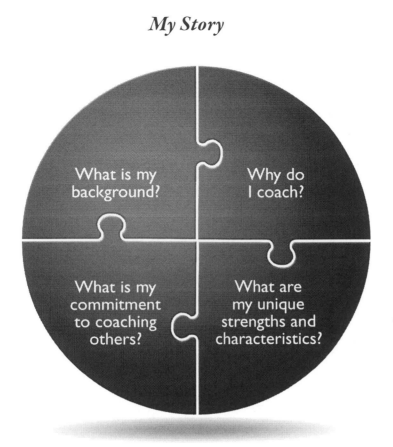

Here is some guidance to walk you through taking the first pass at creating your own story. First, remind yourself why you coach in the first place and what it is that you love about being a coach. Don't edit. Let it roll from there. The people who are meant to be your clients want and need to hear this so they can identify with and relate to you. Get clear on all the reasons you are meant to do what you do.

Remember that your brand is a natural outgrowth of your story—who you are, where you came from, and your passions and experiences to date. Your brand is you. So being able to articulate your story—highlighting what someone really needs to know if they express interest—helps you get known.

For example, a coach who was drawn to coaching female professionals who are moms because of her own struggles and successes as a single working mom can allow that story to infuse her brand. She can become known as the powerhouse coach for working moms who are single or who simply bear the major burden of domestic and parenting responsibilities—because she has credibility, interest, strengths, and passion in this area.

> "Your brand is a natural outgrowth of your story—who you are, where you came from, and your passions and experiences to date."

One last thing. While you are still in the throes of defining your brand and getting your practice started, try to resist the urge to dilute your brand by being all things to all people (this is the same temptation we talked about in the previous module on identifying your niche). This may be challenging as a new coach as it may cause you to give up certain opportunities that don't align with your brand—in the *short*-term, anyway. However, the benefit of focusing all your energy toward the group of clients that most fully appreciate your value—and is prepared to pay for it—will result in much greater results in the long-term.

KEY INSIGHTS

- *Be crystal clear about who you are and what you deliver.*

- *Every sale is an emotional connection based on the ability of the buyer to identify with you.*

- *When you are clear about what differentiates you, you give potential clients the information they need to recognize how you can be uniquely helpful to them.*

- *A brand is a unique promise of value.*

- *Branding is key to being easily identifiable by the people you most want to work with.*

- *Clients need to be exposed to your brand several times before they feel like they know you and before its qualities can be fully absorbed.*

- *Commoditization is mitigated by branding and differentiation.*

Classroom Exercises

Exercise 9-A

What are two words that come to mind when I say Lady Gaga?

_____

_____

What about a Disney movie?

_____

_____

How about Porsche?

_____

_____

Exercise 9-B

Let's capture the essence of your brand in answer to the following questions. Take a few moments to reflect and then write about what comes up.

What five adjectives describe the image and tone you want to set?

_____

_____

What do people think about you?

_____

_____

How do you see yourself?

_____

_____

How do you want to be seen?

_____

_____

What do you want to be known for?

_____

_____

What makes you, and what you offer, unique?

_____

_____

What makes you stand out?

_____

_____

What are three ways you are different, perhaps even offer more value, than other coaches?

_____

_____

Resources

Outline for Your Story (see the following fieldwork)

See Conscious Marketing Model (see Appendix B)

Fieldwork

1.   Share your list of five characteristics from Exercise 9-B with someone who knows you tonight. Ask them whether it resonates for them. Did you forget anything? Can they add anything?

How do you want people to feel after they meet you and read your messages?

_____

_____

What image do you want to project?

_____

_____

What tone do you want to set?

_____

_____

2.   Let's create an outline for your story, answering as many of these questions as feel relevant and natural. This is just the beginning of your story—to get you warmed up.

What is your background?

_____

_____

Why do you coach?

_____

_____

What are your strengths and unique characteristics?

_____

_____

What is your commitment to coaching others?

_____

_____

What do you love about coaching?

_____

_____

What can I expect from you?

_____

_____

OBJECTIVES

*Get clear about the three top
problems your target market faces*

*Learn how to speak in
the language of your target
market so that they know you
are the one for them*

MODULE 10: *What Problems Do You Solve?*

Problems Motivate Spending

People don't wake up in the middle of the night saying, "I need a coach!" More likely, what's keeping them up at night is a problem they cannot solve. How is it that you can get the attention of your target market? Why should someone listen to you in the first place?

Think about what might not be working in the life and career of your ideal clients.

"If I can't figure out how to speak up more powerfully at work, I might get passed over for that promotion."

"If I don't find a soul mate, I'll be alone forever."

"If I don't make more money, I will be stuck in this small studio apartment for ten more years."

Problems might range from managing multiple priorities, to fear of public speaking to transitioning into a leadership role. The types of challenges will vary by target market and it's up to you to identify the top problems your target market faces and be able to speak to them.

People are motivated to buy in order to solve the problems they have—so start your marketing message with a *problem*. Knowing your target market's problems and speaking their problem language helps them identify *you* as the answer to the problem.

What worries does your target market have?

KEY INSIGHTS

- *People buy in terms of the problems that they want to solve.*

- *Positioning yourself as having specific problem-solving expertise gets the attention of your target market.*

Classroom Exercises

What problem, issue, pain, predicament, or challenge(s) are your clients facing that would make them seek assistance? Capture the top three problems each of your target markets face.

Target #1

1.

2.

3.

Target #2

1.

2.

3.

Target #3

1.

2.

3.

Fieldwork

Polish up the list of your target market's top three challenges.

OBJECTIVES

Identify what clients get when they work with you

Be able to clearly articulate the solutions you help facilitate for each problem your clients face

MODULE 11: *What Solutions Do You Bring to Bear?*

Become the Solution

If you as a coach have a solution in the form of a service or program, it is incumbent upon you to communicate that solution to your potential clients. You want to make that solution known; otherwise, you are a well-kept secret and you shortchange yourself and the people who need what you deliver.

You must be able to clearly articulate what people get if they engage with you. Using concise, compelling, and specific language, you must paint a picture of their future after they have worked with you and their issue has been resolved. The questions to mull over are:

- If clients work with you, what will they get as a result?
- What is it that you promise to deliver?
- How will they be better off after working with you?
- What results do you help facilitate when working with clients?
- When you've finished working with clients, what can they expect their condition to be?
- What are the best three things you do for people?

Your possible solutions could include helping clients increase productivity, effectively manage stress, or deal with conflict. Alternately, your solutions might involve helping clients lose weight, become a more effective parent, or increase business revenues (see Appendix G for other sample solutions). What solutions do you provide to your clients?

KEY INSIGHTS

- *Knowing the solution to each of your clients' challenges is key to creating compelling marketing messages.*

Classroom Exercises

Name three specific things you know you can do for people. Don't edit your thoughts. When you're done, go through a second time and tease each solution out to be specific. Replace vague language and jargon with clear, precise verbiage.

Target #1

1.

2.

3.

Target #2

1.

2.

3.

Target #3

1.

2.

3.

Resources

Sample List of Solutions (see Appendix G).

Fieldwork

Polish up the list of solutions you bring to bear.

OBJECTIVES

*Create a concise, memorable
statement that clearly conveys
what you do for people*

MODULE 12: *Your Core Statement*

What Is Your Core Statement?

Your *core statement*, sometimes called an elevator pitch, is your first message about what it is that you do. Your core statement identifies who you serve, what problems you solve, and your solution. It is a ten-second sound bite that succinctly and memorably introduces your services and that answers the question, "What do you do?"

Your core statement focuses on the benefits you provide, spotlights your uniqueness, and must be delivered effortlessly.

The core statement formula I suggest is: target market + problem + solution (T + P + S). We will refer to it as the TPS statement for the remainder of this book. Here is an example core statement:

> I help managers who are leading fractured teams to create collaboration and trust.

In this example, we've got the target market, which is the manager; the problem, which is the fractured team that managers lead; and the solution, which is to create collaboration and trust. You put these three items together, and your core message begins to take shape.

Core Messages

Here are a few more examples of TPS statements to give you more insight into how these can look (see Appendix H for other examples).

> I help emerging leaders who have under-performing employees learn how to engage individuals and build high-performance teams.

> I help couples who argue or shut down communication learn to have constructive conversations to improve their relationship.

> I help people who feel held back in unproductive relationships break the pattern and create meaningful relationships.

To develop your own core statement, you will build on the work you have done in Module 7 (where you defined your target market), Module 10 (where you brainstormed on your target market's top three problems), and Module 11 (where you generated possible solutions that you can provide to these problems). You will take all three of these elements and turn them into a succinct statement that effectively describes the work that you do.

KEY INSIGHTS

- *Your core statement is a quick, easy, and compelling sound bite that informs your clients as to what you deliver in a way that is easy to understand.*

Classroom Exercises

Create one core statement (T + P + S) per target market, as follows (referring back to your notes in Modules 7, 10, and 11 if needed):

T = Who you work with

P = What your clients' problems are

S = The solution your clients can expect

TPS = Target + Problem + Solution

Target Market #1:

Problem:

_____

_____

Solution:

_____

_____

Core Statement (T + P + S):

_____

_____

Target Market #2:

Problem:

_____

_____

Solution:

_____

_____

Core Statement (T + P + S):

_____

_____

Target Market #3:

Problem:

_____

_____

Solution:

_____

_____

Core Statement (T + P + S):

_____

_____

Target Market #4:

Problem:

_____

_____

Solution:

_____

_____

Core Statement (T + P + S):

_____

_____

Share your TPS with your partner. Then, ask your partner to give one minute of feedback:

- How did it land?
- What did you like?
- Did it engage you?
- Did it feel authentic?
- What "feed forward" could you suggest?

Resources

Conscious Marketing Model (see Appendix B) and Sample TPS Core Statements (see Appendix H)

Fieldwork

For each and every target market, finish writing the TPS statements started in class.

TPS for Target Market #1:

_____

_____

TPS for Target Market #2:

_____

_____

TPS for Target Market #3:

_____

_____

Practice saying each one of these messages to a buddy in class. Ask for feedback and then adjust the statement. Practice again. Come fully prepared to read aloud each of your messages in class.

What do you now know about marketing?

_____

_____

What do you now see about marketing yourself that will allow you to move forward with more comfort and ease?

_____

_____

How does this new learning connect with what you've seen about how you used to think, feel, and act with respect to marketing?

_____

_____

What do you see that will help make what you identified to do for yourself even stronger?

_____

_____

OBJECTIVES

*Identify and articulate
the value you deliver*

MODULE 13: *What Value Do You Deliver?*

Your Value Proposition: The Benefits You Deliver

We have discussed the TPS (target-problem-solution) statement as a core foundational element in your conversation with others. It can be thought of as a conversation starter or an answer to an inquiry about what you do for a living.

But, let's say you capture interest, which, after all, is what you are after. What if you have more than ten seconds and your audience demonstrates genuine interest or curiosity?

What is next? What elements might you add that are relevant and that allow your audience to know more about who you are and what you bring to the table?

Essentially, you want to be able to expand on the solutions you deliver. That means fully exploring all the benefits brought about by your solutions—your value proposition. You must be able to speak about each and every one of the benefits clients receive when they work with you if you want to be able to not only capture their interest but to create credibility.

Value can be the obstacles removed, the hurdles jumped, or the opportunities created by delivering your solution. Value is simply an expansion of the results you produce—the end game of the solutions.

How Does Value Fit Into Your Core Message?

Value is the last piece of your core message (Module 12). When you put your target market together with its problem and your solution, you will get to the heart of your value proposition.

Core Messages

When you consider who it is you help (target market), what you help them through (problem), and the solution you provide to address this group's challenges, you have a picture of what *value* you provide.

Another way of phrasing this is to put it into formulaic terms and say that

$$T + P + S \rightarrow V$$

Of course, that way of looking at value is theoretical and meant to help your big-picture understanding. When you get down to actually communicating your core message (the practicalities of marketing), you will want to express your value in terms of the benefits that your solutions provide.

Let's think about what your clients really and fully get in return for their commitment to your practice in time and money. What are the end benefits? What value do you offer them?

KEY INSIGHTS

- *Value is the end benefit(s) of the solutions you deliver.*

- *In order to turn the interest of potential clients into a commitment to work with you, you must be able to speak about the benefits that clients receive when they work with you.*

Classroom Exercises

Make a list of all the value you bring for each solution you cited in Module 12. If it helps your brainstorming process, think of your added value as the end benefits that your solutions deliver.

Fieldwork

Polish up the list of values you began to create in the Classroom Exercise.

OBJECTIVES

Understand the role that storytelling plays in the marketing process

Create the framework for your first client-success story

MODULE 14: *The Role of Storytelling in Marketing*

Background

Stories are powerful tools you can use to communicate without selling. They allow you to share useful information about what you do without having to engage in "sales talk." Storytelling is a natural expression of your marketing messages.

The aim of telling a story is to share a vignette in which you helped a client solve his or her problem in a way that demonstrates your ability to do something similar for your prospective client.

Stories work because they are not intrusive. When you're "selling," for example, you're talking about yourself or interrogating. Neither creates a safe space for relationship building or intimacy to occur. In fact, you might offend or bore the client or be making a very unattractive "pitch" in such cases.

In contrast, sharing a success story lets you reveal information about your competence without pressure, hyperbole, or cliché. It offers a chance to demonstrate how your talent and the services you offer provide a real solution to your prospective client's real problem.

Crafting Your Story

It is important that your story focuses on results, not on what coaching is and how it works. People do not buy definitions of coaching or explanations of how your coaching process works. They buy results. Here are some examples of client stories that focus on results and solutions.

> "I worked with a senior leader [target market] who had been passed over for a promotion two years in a row [problem]. Together we uncovered the two biggest stumbling blocks to her advancement and created a plan to increase her confidence and skill sets in those areas. Within nine months, she improved her communication skills and increased her executive presence to get the promotion she sought [solution]! She is now enjoying the corner office and has received a raise and title commensurate with her contribution."

> "I had the pleasure of working with a stay-at-home dad [target market] who was missing having a creative outlet and extra cash [problem]. Together, we figured out how to launch his freelance writing career so that he could keep his hand in the work world while still being there for his two daughters when they got home from elementary school [solution]. He and his wife now feel less economic pressure, he has an outlet for his creativity, and he feels more fulfilled as a person."

With storytelling, you articulate the solution you offer to each person. That starts with knowing the top problems that motivate your clients into action.

We said before that people do not wake up in the middle of the night saying, "I need a coach!" Instead, they stay awake thinking things like: "I need to make more money," "I'm completely out of shape," "If I don't straighten out my team, I risk getting down-sized," or "If I don't find a relationship, I'll grow old alone." You get it. It's gremlin talk.

So practice weaving the top problems—and your solutions—into a powerful, well-rehearsed story about a person you helped. Your story should demonstrate that you have a clear understanding of the nature of the client's challenge, that you have helped someone solve this challenge before, and that you're capable of supporting the client to solve a similar challenge.

Client Story

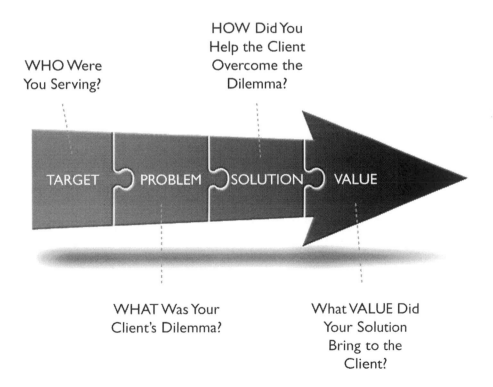

The goal of storytelling is to start creating trust and to establish credibility. You set the stage for the person to identify with the story and see him or herself benefiting from the results you bring. The client now knows that you *understand* his or her goals and roadblocks and, more importantly, that you are able to help bring about positive results when faced with the same or similar goals or impediments.

Your overall aim is to engage in a natural conversation, very lightly sprinkled with stories that allow for the client to start to know, like, and trust you. This will help the prospective client see you as competent, resourceful, and capable. It builds trust, which is a precursor to building a relationship.

> "Once stories become a foundational part of how you talk about what coaching can create, you will experience a new level of ease in marketing."

Once stories become a foundational part of how you talk about what coaching can create, you will experience a new level of ease in marketing. (Tip: It is important to end any client-success story with a question so that you get the client to start thinking about his or her situation, for example, "What types of challenges do you face?")

Formula for Client-Success Story

As you begin to construct your own client-success stories, consider your target market, the problems you have helped to solve, the solutions that the clients have experienced, and the value of these solutions to your clients.

Note: If your inner critic starts talking—telling you that you don't have any successes yet because you're just starting out—I want you to observe those negative thoughts and beliefs and then let them go. Focus instead on mentally scrolling through the people you have helped, like characters on a movie screen. Once you have this mental (or written) list compiled, you can note the more evident ways in which you have supported them. Then move on to the more subtle ways you may have helped them. Also consider the ways in which you have supported your pro bono and classmate clients thus far; these coaching experiences might also be transferable to alternate situations. Suddenly, your universe of marketable successes will grow!

The truth is this: you didn't wake up and just like that decide to become a coach and then enroll for this program and pick up this book. You have had this desire and talent within you before you had even a word for it. Perhaps you were the family mediator or volunteered as a Big Brother or Sister. Maybe you were the one all your girlfriends came to for advice on dating. Perhaps you were the matchmaker, the good listener, or the font of useful resources. Somehow, somewhere, you have been showing up as a coach before stepping into this classroom.

You are here because coaching is your calling. Now, think again about who you have helped and what occurred for them as a result of your listening, your asking questions, and your providing resources.

By exploring these questions and linking their answers together in coherent stories, you have within you compelling stories for letting potential clients know what you do in a way that is natural, informative, and *authentic*.

KEY INSIGHTS

- *Stories allow you to communicate naturally without selling.*

- *Stories demonstrate that you have an understanding of issues relevant to your prospective client, you have worked in the past with a client to solve a similar issue, and you are capable of doing the same with the prospective client.*

- *Stories set the stage for establishment of trust and credibility.*

Classroom Exercises

Create an outline for a powerful client story using the following questions.

1. The target market: *Whom* were you serving?

_____

_____

_____

2. The problem you solved: *What* was your client's dilemma?

_____

_____

_____

3. The solution you delivered: *How* did you help the client overcome the dilemma?

_____

_____

_____

4. *What* additional *value* did your solution bring to this client?

_____

_____

_____

Resources

Student Samples to Inspire Your Storytelling (see Appendix I)

Fieldwork

Polish up your client-success story using the questions posed above.

OBJECTIVES

*Understand the role credibility
and trust play in getting
the client to "yes"*

*Explore ways to build
credibility and trust*

*Be able to naturally talk about
what makes you credible
and trustworthy*

MODULE 15: *Credibility and Trust: Getting the Client to "Yes"*

Background

Here is the reality: Consumers buy from people they know, like, and trust. For someone to say yes to your services, that person needs to spend time with you (i.e., know you) to learn about what makes you credible and trustworthy.

The most effective way you can do this is to establish a genuine relationship with potential clients. Just as it is highly unlikely for someone you first meet to agree to marry you without knowing you, it is unlikely that people will invest in you and your services without building rapport and trust that is built over time.

Your job is to build a relationship with your potential clients so that they can get to know you and what you stand for. You create a relationship as you prepare them to say yes to you and the solutions you bring to bear. The ultimate result is that you both win. I like to say that conscious marketing is commerce with connection.

As Sherven and Sniechowski noted in *The Heart of Marketing*,

> Marketing is the process of taking your customers down a particular path at the end of which is an anticipated sale. But that sale is

usually not immediate. It takes between three to nine impressions before someone buys, so all you can do is prepare the way so that your potential client grows to know, like, and trust you.

In order for the client to develop trust and discover your credibility, it is key that the client has several positive experiences of you. These experiences will lead the client to a strong sense that you are honest and help the client see that you are competent. These experiences will also help the client discover coaching as a viable modality.

In all, credibility and trustworthiness boil down to your integrity, capability, and results.

Building Credibility and Trust

Get in Front of the Client. Being seen and heard is the starting point for building credibility. It establishes you in the minds of others as someone who can possibly solve their problem. So, first, you must get your message out. After you get in front of the people you feel are the best fit for you, you can then offer them a "free" taste of your character and abilities, so they can experience what it would be like to work with you. You can then let your integrity and capacity to achieve results speak for you. As clients begin to see the positive results from their interactions with you, your credibility builds.

> "Your job is to build a relationship with your potential clients so that they can get to know you and what you stand for."

Be Present. Being present is the foundation for creating intimacy and trust. Your listening skills, language, passion, knowledge, and authenticity all contribute toward creating presence. We have all had an experience where we felt connected to and inspired by someone we just met because they were being present (and authentic) with us. You know you are present when both parties are at ease, comfortable, and interested in the conversation. While writing and speaking can pave the way toward building client trust, it all "clicks" when you are actively engaged with someone through listening and dialogue. Being present means you are listening *for* the other person and *to* the other person, and contributing to the exchange from a place of knowledge and passion—not just talking about you and your services.

Be Consistent. Reliability, reputation, and consistency are cornerstones of being trusted in the marketplace. Clear and confident communication demonstrates these qualities to others. In other words, you have to say what you mean and mean what you say. Simple. Direct. True. Inconsistency in your follow-through or execution will undermine all your effort. Your actions must match your commitment, and you should strive to "over deliver" every time.

> "When you genuinely want others to win and when you enjoy helping them do that, you inspire authentic trust."

Be Intentional. Intention is having an agenda. In the case of marketing, the agenda is for you to help your client feel and understand that you genuinely want the client to reach his or her desired outcome. When you genuinely want others to win and when you enjoy helping them do that, you inspire authentic trust. What you say and how you act is the manifestation of your agenda. The behavior that best establishes your intentions and inspires trust is acting in the best interest of others. When people know you "have their back," they will naturally trust you.

Remember Your Story

In order to be truly present, consistent, and intentional—on purpose—you've got to have a quiet yet strong belief in yourself. You have to *feel* credible to *be* credible. Is it possible that your inner critic might be speaking so loudly that you have begun to believe that being "new" to coaching mitigates your efficacy?

One of the best ways to build up your confidence and manage your gremlin is to know why you are uniquely qualified to do this work. This is why you constructed your story in Module 9 (e.g., your background, how you got into coaching, why you love coaching, etc.) and why I encourage you to go over your story again and again until it becomes completely natural for you to speak about.

Preparation, in this case, is a great antidote to fear, doubt, and worry. The last thing you want to do when asked about your background is stammer or, worse yet, come across as though you are reading your resume.

As you share your story with your audience, you will notice something. Your confidence will start to soar and it's no wonder why! When you reconnect to your source, your passion, and your purpose, you re-ignite. It is this place that you want to write and speak from. It is this place that will allow your credibility to shine through.

Trust does not exist in a vacuum. It is only when you are *credible, present, consistent, intentional*, and *grounded in your story* that you generate the flow that inspires people to work with you. When you are conscious to these qualities and manifest them in your interactions with others, it creates a fertile ground for trust to flourish. You become a magnet for those you are meant to work with.

KEY INSIGHTS

- *In order to buy your services, people first need to know, like, and trust you.*

- *In order to build trust with your potential clients, you must focus on building credibility, while being present, consistent, and intentional.*

- *Trust and credibility are key to a sale.*

- *Get clear for yourself as to why you are credible and qualified to help others create their futures. Reconnecting with your story will help you do that.*

Classroom Exercises

List out every reason you are qualified to do your coaching work. Go back as far in time as you can remember.

_____

_____

_____

_____

_____

How can you establish credibility and trust without boring the prospect or hard-selling yourself—neither playing small nor grandiose?

_____

_____

_____

_____

_____

Fieldwork

Finish the classroom exercise above. List out every reason you are qualified to do this work, and continue brainstorming on how you can establish credibility and trust with the client.

OBJECTIVES

Learn how to move a client along the path where he or she comes to know, like, and trust you

Discover what constitutes an effective offer

Create three offers you can invite people to partake in

MODULE 16: *Offers: How to Give People a Taste of Your Value*

Background

There is always a next step. As marketers, it is our job to create a safe opening for that next step to occur naturally. The invitation to take that step needs to be specific, clear, and appropriate given the level of interest the client has demonstrated.

We call this step many things: making an offer, a call to action, or a pink spoon (think of the sampler spoons used by Baskin Robbins to give people a taste of their ice cream in the hope that they will buy more).

People want a taste of what you deliver before they make a decision. An offer or pink spoon gives them a sampling of what it might be like to work with you.

With an effective offer, you can increase your ability to get to yes.

The Offer, Explored

Offers can take a variety of forms. For example:

- Take my assessment!
- Come hear me speak.

- Come to a free informational teleclass I'm giving.
- Read my article and let me know what you think.
- Can we keep in touch via email?
- Would you like to test drive a coaching session?
- Check out my website.
- Check out my blog.
- May I send you my monthly newsletter?
- Friend me on Linked In, Facebook, Plaxo, etc.

These are just some of the options available, with room for many more, limited only by your creativity, interest level, and areas of expertise.

What makes an offer effective? Effective offers:

- are delivered professionally
- are framed using attention-getting language for the target market
- make a clear call to action that flows naturally
- address a problem of your target market
- deliver exceptional value
- serve as the first of many offers.

An effective offer is one that resonates with the prospective client. It is one that the prospect feels pulled toward, and perhaps even compelled, to take action around. You will need to have a few offers in your toolbox so that you can make an appropriate offer based on a prospect's level of interest. Accordingly, offers can range from requiring little to significant commitment on the person's part. (Think of an ice cream store that offers both a free taste of ice cream and a special to "buy a gallon, get a gallon free.")

A low-commitment coaching offer might involve asking individuals to friend you on Facebook, exchange business cards, or to check out your website. Medium commitment might involve asking if you can send an article that you wrote on a topic just discussed to get their feedback or asking them if they would like to take your free online assessment. High commitment could be offering them a gratis session to test drive what coaching with you might be like.

My Client Offers

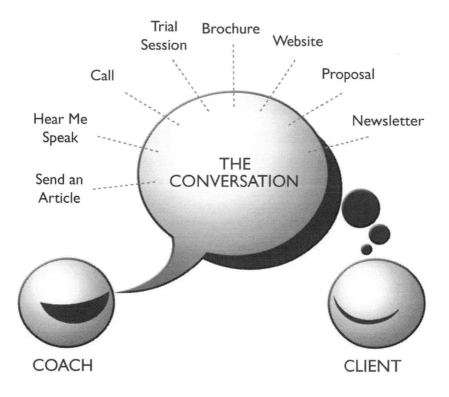

Your creativity, expertise, and talents will drive your choice of offers; you can also customize your offers to different individuals or groups, based on their unique needs and challenges.

KEY INSIGHTS

- *You must invite people to take the next step with you.*

- *Effective offers increase your ability to get someone to experience you and to therefore say yes.*

Classroom Exercises

How might you give clients a taste of what it would be like to work with you? Let's brainstorm a list of ways you could invite them to do, see, hear, taste, read, and experience your services.

_____

_____

_____

_____

_____

_____

_____

_____

Resources

Sample Offers (see Appendix J)

Fieldwork

Can you think of one offer for each of the following categories?

Low commitment:

_____

_____

_____

_____

Medium commitment:

_____

_____

_____

_____

High commitment:

_____

_____

_____

_____

OBJECTIVES

*Learn what stands between you
and setting the rates you deserve*

*Create conscious thinking to
support you in communicating
about your fees*

MODULE 17: *Rate Packaging*

Background

"So, what do you charge?"

Did you just cringe?

When this question emerges from the mouth of a potential client, many coaches can't hear over the cacophony of gremlin choruses reaching crescendo pitch. Their inability to remain conscious when the topic of money comes up lessens their ability to set rates that honor their value and that create sustainability for their business.

Let's explore some popular money mindsets (aka gremlin scripts) one by one and see what's *really* going on.

Money Mindsets, Dispelled

"I Don't Have Enough Experience to Charge More." Really? How many hours did you train? How much did your training cost in time and money? And, I'm curious, how many hours *are* enough? What is the magic number that will have you thinking you are finally "there"? Aren't you always learning? Isn't that the nature of your profession? You don't need to charge low rates simply because you are still learning and "in process."

As coaches, we get paid to learn and give away what we're learning in real time. Learning makes us *more valuable* to our clients—it does not *under-value* us. As with all limiting thoughts, you have to shift your mindset. Instead of seeing your desire and need for professional development as evidence of not having arrived, see how it creates *more* value.

Eckhart Tolle says that the spirit-filled teacher never thinks she's ready; she feels that there's always something more to learn. I don't know about you, but I do my best work when I am engaged in professional development. I am on fire when I'm learning, and I give my best as a result.

"Who Am I to Charge More Than Other Coaches?" Don't look at everybody else's rates because they're all looking at yours and almost everyone is undercharging as a result. It's a disempowering cycle. Break the chain.

> "The inability of many coaches to remain conscious when the topic of money comes up lessens their ability to set rates that honor their value and that create sustainability for their business."

In terms of hard dollars and soft benefits, gauge the impact of your solution in your client's life and business. What is the value of finding a soul mate or getting one's business into high gear? What does the client get? What is that worth? That's how much you charge!

"*I* Wouldn't Pay That Much." First off, I don't believe you. If you really thought that, would you have forked over thousands of dollars for coach training? You know for a fact that you would pay for a desired outcome that was important to you. Guess what? That means others would too. Besides, what price is "too much" for someone who wants to manifest a dream?

"My Clients Can't Afford to Pay That." Now you're thinking for your clients. Our code of ethics states that we honor clients' ability to think for themselves. But you are deciding for your clients how they should spend their money. If rate setting were a coach competency, you just failed because you set an agenda for the client!

As coaches, we don't give people fish; we teach them how to fish. As practitioners of self-directed learning, it is our charter to allow clients to make their own decisions about what they spend and where. Our clients are responsible for their own financial decisions. Period.

I hear you pushing back. What about the client who just got laid off and for whom money is an issue? When money is tight, it might be time to re-assess non-essential expenditures like fancy dinners or a luxury vacation, but not the very thing that will ensure a person's ability to get back on track! It is presumptuous and dangerous to decide for someone else that he or she can't afford to get back into the driver's seat to create an income!

Besides, if you make that decision for your clients and charge less than your service is worth, just think of the example you're setting for your clients. You're literally robbing them of the opportunity to be inspired to recognize and claim *their* value!

"Who Am I to Charge More Than (My Mentor, Colleagues, What Others Tell Me)?" What's at play here is comparison, but comparison is only valuable if you're comparing the right things! Since practically everyone undercharges, if you follow along like a sheep, then you too will undercharge. The only worthy comparison to make is that which exists between your confidence and the value of the results that clients will get from working with you.

If you're going to charge what your service is worth, you have to change your thinking. You have to create a new mindset based on value—return on investment. Then, and only then, will you be of most value to your clients.

Do you know what stands in the way of claiming your value? What is it going to take for you to set rates that reflect your contribution? Give yourself permission to accept these new paradigms. And, hey, start charging what you're worth!

Lowering and Raising Fees

Never lower your fee without removing a service or value. The client must view fee as an investment. Be prepared to speak to the return on investment or experience rather than fee. The time to raise fees is when the client's perception of value increases.

How to Talk About Rates

When people ask about your fees, you may be tempted to focus on the actual cost. While the numbers are important, keep in mind that what matters most for anyone is the value that they will be receiving in return for their investment. In other words, people can wrap their heads around and start to feel more comfortable talking about money when you as the service provider can concretely articulate exactly what they get for their investment. It helps them visualize and identify with the result they want. It creates clarity and that is a superb platform for decision-making.

For example: "Using the 'Reach Your NOI Program,' I have helped business leaders achieve an increase in their net operating income of 10% within six months."

By focusing on the value, rather than price, you make it easier for potential clients to get to yes. Also note that the goal is to get clients to say yes once and retain them for a long period. Why? If they stay longer, they get much better results and they tell more people. You, in turn, get more referrals, which increases brand visibility and revenue. Well thought out rate setting contributes to creating a sustainable business model where everyone feels good and wins.

It also creates ease in speaking about fees, which keeps the gremlins in their cages.

Rate-Packaging Options

Every client is unique in that each has his or her own money fears, insecurities, and capacity to pay. It makes sense, then, to create a few options to accommodate various mindsets and budgetary "needs."

Some people dive right into the pool of coaching, while others like to dip their toe in the water first. Sometimes, it's a matter of ability to commit or to find time; other times, it's a matter of budget and what they perceive they can afford at the time. Whatever it is, it is helpful to give options to keep clients thinking and evaluating. Just hearing a price can shut down your brain, but knowing there are options, you are more likely to listen for what suits you. Think of all the options at Starbucks. Can you imagine if there were just one type of drink offered on the menu and it cost six dollars? You might not visit Starbucks a second time.

> "If you're going to charge what your service is worth, you have to create a new mindset based on value—return on investment."

To address differing client needs, I suggest creating three different options at three different price points—more than three is cumbersome to talk about and confusing for people to take in. Again, using Starbucks as an example, I might describe my favorite drink order twice to a new friend but when she tries to order the same thing, it might still come back wrong. Why? The type of bean, temperature, size, style, strength, and flavors are hard for our brain to take in all at once when new. The same happens when talking about pricing. Make your price packages easy to talk about and digest. The simpler the better.

- Creating options will help clients who have more and less abundant mindsets pick the one that is right for them.
- Providing your clients options will lessen the fear and real possibility of charging too little or too much. They will choose as much as they can mentally and literally afford and you didn't give anything away as you are clear as to the packages value and each is different in material ways that can be equated to dollars and sense/cents.
- With options in play, the client can process the value he or she will derive from each option, thereby giving you an opportunity to discuss the value, not the price.

Clients actually don't care as much about rates as they care about the results that they get for their money. It is therefore incumbent upon you to clearly and succinctly articulate all of the solutions you help facilitate and the value they get from each. Then, estimate what each is worth and you have your fee schedule.

KEY INSIGHTS

- *Fear degrades your ability to set and ask for the rates that you deserve. Getting conscious and creating new mindsets positions you to charge what you are worth.*

- *Clients believe you have more value when you value yourself appropriately. It is natural to value what costs more.*

- *Offering options allows you to change the conversation from price to value.*

- *You will attract the clients you are meant to work with.*

- *Charging the rate you want will create what is needed for the life you want to lead and the kind of work you want to do. You can now do and give more to every client, thereby enhancing your results and getting more clients.*

Classroom Exercises

What stands in the way of claiming your value?

_____

_____

_____

_____

What is it going to take for you to set rates that reflect your contribution?

_____

_____

_____

_____

Resources

Sample Rate Packaging (see Appendix K)

Million Dollar Consulting: The Professionals Guide to Growing a Practice by Alan Weiss (see Chapter 9)

Fieldwork

Create a few different price points in your offerings. Name your options so that you can refer to them without actually using the dollar amounts. Tip: Make it irresistible to go for the high option.

OBJECTIVES

Understand the prospect universe

*Be able to quickly determine who is
ready for coaching and who is not*

*Learn how to successfully interact
with the four client mindsets*

*Understand how a client
mindset should inform your
marketing strategy*

MODULE 18: *Qualifying People in a Conversation: Knowing Who Is Ready*

Background

How many prospective coaching clients await you? The universe of potential prospects is narrow yet many coaches scatter their seeds widely.

In fact only about 5% of the people you encounter will be genuine prospects so you must carefully target your marketing efforts. You would get turned down 95 times out of 100 if you did not. If we randomly market, only 5 people out of 10 would say yes.

Steve Mitten, the former president of the International Coach Federation and author of *Marketing Essentials for Coaches* (2003) has noted,

> If you carefully select your prospects to be within the most likely age and income distribution, at least one to two in six individuals would be open, willing and able to work with you (5%). If you develop a niche, this can increase to one in three.

Although it's difficult to identify with precision how many potential clients exist for interested coaches, calculations by Mitten have put the number at only 400 to 800 prospects per coach. Remember, we're talking about prospective clients, those who might want to work with you but haven't signed the dotted line yet. Clearly, you need to know what you're doing when you start seeking clients—they are not going to ring your doorbell. Finding clients will take time, effort, and conscious strategy.

Did you know that it takes *three to five hours of marketing* to find *one* paying client? Yet, you only have a certain number of hours per year to find these clients to fill your practice (and remember that these clients only make up 5% of the population). If you target the wrong people (the other 95%), you will not meet your marketing goal and, frankly, you may be out of business. In order to spend your marketing time wisely, you need to be able to differentiate a good prospect from a bad one—quickly—and you must resist the urge to serve everyone who comes your way.

> "Only about 5% of the people you encounter will be genuine prospects so you must carefully target your marketing efforts."

What are the implications of Mitten's facts? First, you cannot afford to waste time. Second, you must learn how to qualify prospects effectively. If you do not, you may lose valuable opportunities. The moral of this story? You need to make marketing a priority, and you need to make the time you spend on marketing count.

Understanding Potential Clients' Mindsets to Qualify Leads

If only 5% of the individuals out there will ultimately be interested in your coaching services, it can be helpful to understand how best to recognize this relatively small group of individuals. Understanding the following four mindsets of potential clients—growth, trouble, even keel, and overconfident—will help you focus in on those who are primed for coaching and those who are not.

Expansion Mindset. The individual in a growth or expansion mindset feels that the gap between his or her reality and his or her desired outcome can be closed if something is gained, achieved, increased, or improved. This individual will be receptive to hiring a coach if you can show that coaching can make it possible to close this gap.

Trouble Mindset. An individual with a trouble mindset also sees a discrepancy, but this time it is a discrepancy on the down side. Something has caused a negative deviation, and the person is open to solutions that promise to help close the gap. This person is receptive to hiring a coach if you can demonstrate that coaching can help close this gap.

> "The aim is to ask questions that help you determine whether a positive or negative discrepancy exists (expansion or trouble mindset, respectively). Remember, no discrepancy, no sale."

Even-Keel Mindset. This individual does not perceive any discrepancy between current reality and his or her desired outcome. He or she is content with how things are and has no motivation or incentive to change. The individual doesn't want to rock his or her boat. Therefore, the probability of this individual engaging you as a coach is pretty low. Typically, if there is no gap, there is no sale. So just keep in touch until a discrepancy emerges. In time, it will, and if you have been there consistently demonstrating your value, when the time is right, you will get that call.

Overconfident Mindset. The overconfident individual perceives reality as being far better than what he or she expected and is therefore unreceptive to any proposals that point at change. Your chance of changing this person's mind is practically nil. Walk away. Simply keep in touch until such time that a discrepancy arises. Life being what it is, one will emerge, and if you are there, having built a good relationship, you are well positioned.

There are questions that you can ask a prospect to help determine which mindset he or she is in at any given time. Here are a few:

- What are your top challenges? How are you feeling about that?
- What are you working toward in your career? relationship? etc.?
- What is next for you?
- Where are you with X?

Which questions might you ask to uncover current reality and a prospective client's desired future state?

As we coaches know, when we ask open-ended questions about an individual's current reality, we have an opportunity to learn about the person's current challenges and successes. When we ask about the individual's vision for the future, any gap that might exist between where he or she is and where he or she wants to be will come into focus.

The aim is to ask questions that help you determine whether a positive or negative discrepancy exists (expansion or trouble mindset, respectively). Remember, no discrepancy, no sale. Just keep in touch and build credibility, trust, and relationship over time for when the person does need your services.

KEY INSIGHTS

- *There are four mindsets that a prospect can have at any given time: expansion, trouble, even keel, and overconfident.*

- *Each mindset is indicative of a client's readiness—or lack thereof—for coaching.*

- *Each mindset can be used to inform whether and how to take marketing action.*

- *Do not expect to make a sale to a person with an even-keel or overconfident mindset. These individuals will eventually come full circle. Just keep in touch.*

Classroom Exercises

Exercise 18-A

Which questions might you ask to uncover current reality and a prospective client's desired future state?

_____

_____

_____

Exercise 18-B

What offers (e.g., check out my blog, take my assessment, Friend me on Facebook) are appropriate for each of these response modes? For a reminder of offer types, see Module 16.

Expansion:

_____

_____

_____

Trouble:

_____

_____

_____

_____

Even-keel:

_____

_____

_____

Overconfident:

_____

_____

_____

Fieldwork

Continue to think and write about which offers are appropriate for each of the response modes.

Expansion:

_____

_____

_____

Trouble:

_____

_____

_____

_____

Even-keel:

_____

_____

_____

Overconfident:

_____

_____

_____

OBJECTIVES

Discover how to naturally invite someone to work with you

Create an outline script for inviting someone to a trial session

Create two ways you can ask someone to engage in a coaching relationship

MODULE 19: *How to Invite a Client Into a Coaching Relationship*

Background

Having some ideas about what you could say to invite someone to test a coaching session may help you feel more at ease when the time arises. So let's talk about how you might invite someone to do either.

Trial Sessions

Let's say you meet someone whom you think represents your ideal client and whom shows genuine curiosity in coaching but doesn't ask to sign up with you. Because you'd like to have this person in your practice, you decide you'd like to offer them a trial session. How might you do that? What might you say? Here are a couple of examples.

> "I'd like to offer you a gratis one-hour session to explore that issue with you and see if my thinking partnership could help."

> "I'd love to help you achieve that goal and would like to offer you a one-hour session at no charge to explore whether coaching with me might be for you."

Speak from your heart and say what you genuinely feel. If you stay connected to your enthusiasm for working with this client as well as your sincere interest in helping him or her, you will find that your ability to offer a trial session will flow naturally.

Coaching Engagements

Let's pretend that the prospective client has had a trial session with you. You have now come to the close of that session and you want to invite the client to sign up for your services. How do you ask the prospective client if he or she would like to work with you? Here are a couple of examples.

> "That's quite a powerful vision you have for your future. If you're serious about realizing it, I would love to be your coach."

> "I really enjoyed coaching you and would love to support you in making your dream a reality."

Again, if your goal is to be authentic, just say what you really feel and desire and put it out there. No gimmicks, no deadlines, no pushing. Simply make a genuine offer based on your sincere desire to work with the individual and wait for the client to respond in a way that feels right for him or her.

If the client has an expansion or a trouble mindset, you may see him or her sign on with you. If the client has an even-keel or overconfident mindset, you may simply have to wait until another time when something shifts for the client. Nonetheless, you will have likely made a meaningful connection and planted a seed for future coaching work.

KEY INSIGHTS

- *Knowing what you might say in order to invite someone to engage with you will help you feel more at ease when the time actually arises.*

- *The key to inviting someone to work with you is to get present, speak from the heart, and stay in integrity with a healthy dose of detachment.*

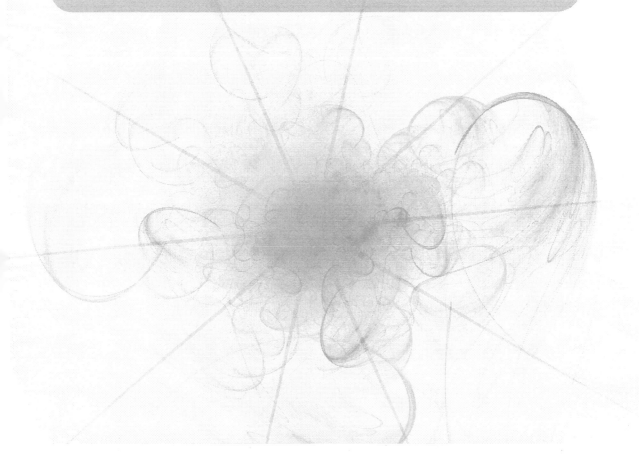

Classroom Exercises

Exercise 19-A: Trial Session

You meet someone whom you think represents your ideal client and whom shows real curiosity in coaching but who doesn't ask to sign up with you. Because you'd like to have this person in your practice, you decide you'd like to offer them a trial session.

Write out your offer to do a trial session:

_____

_____

_____

_____

_____

_____

_____

_____

_____

Exercise 19-B: Coaching Engagement

Think of two ways you can ask for business that are authentic for you.

1.

_____

_____

_____

_____

_____

_____

2.

_____

_____

_____

_____

_____

_____

Fieldwork

Polish up both invitations to invite someone to work with you.

OBJECTIVES

Learn about the common objections you will face

Explore several options for responding to an objection

Practice how to respond with integrity and authenticity when a potential client does not want to engage in coaching

MODULE 20: *Where to Go From "No"?*

Background

The top three objections you are bound to face are about time, money, and trust. They may sound something like this:

"I don't have the money right now," or "Money is tight."

"I need time to think about this."

"We'll see. I don't know enough yet."

If you face these objections, you can respond in many ways. The key is to find a way that feels authentic for you. This is not a matter of following a script or of copying what works for me or any other marketing teacher. It's a matter of connecting with your own natural voice and responding in a way that feels true to you, your beliefs, and your style.

As a coach you want to feel genuine and authentic. So, when you hear client objections, the part of you that doesn't want to sound "sales-y" may automatically want to fold and go silent. But the two are not mutually exclusive: you can be genuine and authentic while still proactively responding to your clients' objections.

It is about getting present, checking in with your beliefs and values, and responding from that place. A healthy dose of detachment can also help you respond to objections in a constructive and comfortable way.

Some options to think over to get your thinking started on how to respond to client objections are shown below.

Affordability

Oftentimes, a client will assert that his or her financial situation is an impediment to hiring you as a coach. In such a case, it is important to actively listen, let the client know you have heard him or her, and then, if you feel good about proceeding, ask permission before engaging in further dialogue. For example:

> "I am hearing that this does not fit your budget, yet you see tremendous value in coaching with me. Is that right?" (If yes, proceed. If no, ask the person to clarify his or her feelings and position.)

> "Is it alright to explore this with you further?" (If yes, proceed. If no, stop there and honor the person's boundary.)

> "You can be genuine and authentic while still proactively responding to your clients' objections."

> "May I explore with you what the cost to you is if you do not take action now? What do you stand to gain if you do solve this dilemma? What is that worth to you?

> I would love to support you in being able to give this gift to yourself. Might I help you explore ways in which this might work?" (If yes, proceed.)

"May I share some options that other clients have taken advantage of when they found themselves in a similar situation?"

Remember, this is just an example of dialogue that *could* occur. It is not a scripted recommendation. It is instead one possibility that I have used successfully in the past when the circumstances have lent themselves to it. I am comfortable engaging in this way with people. Being bold but gentle is part of my brand and therefore I am being authentic when I take this approach.

Someone else with a softer approach might try a similar response but instead say something like...

"Before we focus on cost, I'd like to ask you, what do you stand to *gain* if you solve this dilemma? I see. What is that worth to you?

A harder question—but one worth exploring—is, what is the cost to you if you do not take action now?"

This tweak is small but significant as this approach avoids beginning with the dramatic question of cost, saving that for *after* an exploration of value has taken place. Some coaches might prefer the more intense questioning; others might prefer to ease into that challenging question with a more positive starting focus on value.

The key is to be genuine in what you say and do, finding an approach that feels authentic while also helping the client dig a little deeper into the objection. If you feel like you are being invasive, step back, take a breath, and regroup. Being conscious means pausing to get clear enough to follow your instincts.

If a client is meant to be yours, all you need to do is pave the path for the client to come your way. If it is not meant to be, there is nothing you can say to make it happen.

Need More Time

When a client says he or she needs more time, it typically means one of two things: (a) she is not ready yet for coaching in the *short-term* but may be open to it in the near or mid-term future or (b) she sees no need for coaching in the long-term or foreseeable future.

Let's start with the last case first. Here, either the client does not perceive a gap between what he or she wants to achieve and where he or she is today or the person thinks he or she has got it all handled. Remember the even-keel and overconfident mindsets? That's what's happening here. If you sense that a client sees no need for coaching now or in the foreseeable future, you can walk away for now, always keeping the door open for the future by keeping in contact with the person. There is little value in overtly pursuing this conversation at this juncture.

> "Honor clients who express that they need more time. Show respect by leaving the door open to working together in the future, when the time is right and the need arises."

Sometimes, though, when clients say that they need more time to think about coaching, it means that they are not ready to commit in the short-term but they may be ready a few months or so down the line. They still recognize a gap in their lives or have a desire for something more and can see the value of coaching, just not right away.

The client's reluctance in this case might just indicate a busy lifestyle, a certain personality style, or a desire to continue reflecting on personal and professional needs. In this case, you can ask the client for permission to check in with him or her in a few weeks or ask for a time frame that feels right.

Honor clients who express that they need more time. Show respect by leaving the door open to working together in the future, when the time is right and the need arises.

Don't Know Enough Yet

The third common objection can come in the form of "I don't know enough about you just yet." If you sense or know that the prospect has not had repeated exposure to you yet (at least three times), plan to keep in contact. Conscious marketers are always thinking about opportunities to connect with future clients to build credibility through relationship. This is where having a "keep in touch" strategy comes into play. Stay on the client's radar in a way that allows the real you to become known. Nothing can replace real connection in paving a path to alignment. A sale is simply that—aligning the client's needs with appropriate solutions.

In sum, when you invite a potential client to engage your coaching services, wait and see how he or she responds. Take a deep breath and speak from an authentic place, while respecting the client where he or she is at the time. Maybe that means exploring the costs and benefits of coaching versus no coaching; maybe that means offering up more information on coaching; or maybe that means giving the client the space to walk away until a perceived need for coaching arises. Regardless, by staying connected to your values and not getting overly attached to a particular client or a particular outcome, you can handle coaching objections in a way that maximizes your opportunity to secure clients—now and in the future.

KEY INSIGHTS

- *The key to managing objections from potential clients is to stay in integrity and be authentic in how you respond.*

- *Be willing to walk away when a client is not interested or ready. A healthy sense of detachment is key in being able to do this.*

- *Always stay connected to your potential clients should they become receptive to working with you.*

Classroom Exercises

Find a partner in class and take turns role-playing the following scenarios.

Scenario #1: You meet someone who you think represents your ideal client profile and who shows real curiosity in coaching but doesn't ask to sign up with you. Because you'd like to have this person in your practice, you decide you'd like to offer a trial session.

Scenario #2: You've come to the end of a trial session with a prospective client and the client asks about your fee. After you provide the client with an answer, the prospect says:

1. "Ouch. I can't afford that."

2. "I'm not ready to take that on. I have a lot on my plate right now."

3. "I'm not sure about all of this. We just met."

Fieldwork

Ask a classmate if he or she would be willing to practice with you. Continue to role-play the three scenarios outlined above, with your partner.

OBJECTIVES

Understand what a marketing plan accomplishes

Figure out where and how to locate your ideal clients

Select three ways, best suited to you, to connect with your ideal clients

Create your written marketing plan

MODULE 21: *How to Create a Simple Yet Impactful Marketing Plan*

Background

A *marketing plan* is a strategy that outlines what you will do, with whom, and when you will take action. It is a blueprint for how you will build your client base.

Later on in the program, we will create a personal action plan, which is simply a subset of your marketing plan. It chunks down the specific tasks embedded within each strategy and specifies when you will take each of these steps.

The marketing plan answers these questions:

- Where do I meet these people? (e.g., at industry networking events, meetings for new-moms groups, the career office of college campuses, on the Internet through the Twitter community)
- How do I meet these people? (e.g., during cocktail hour, while delivering free workshops, at open-chat sessions, by posting useful Tweets to special-interest groups)
- What preparation needs to occur in order to enable these meetings to occur? (e.g., do I need a business card, a Twitter account, a brochure?)

Note that there is a real people-based focus when it comes to marketing your coaching practice. Unlike a product that you can create a glossy photo of or pay others to give out as free samples to people walking by, there is no substitute for you.

The marketing plan can be thought of as a blueprint for building your practice. Unlike the personal action plan, which involves creating your to-do items and scheduling them at the "ground" level (we'll learn more in Module 23), the marketing plan is much more high level. You will be strategizing on who you want to meet, and where (the venues in which you can meet them), leaving the nuts and bolts to-do items of executing that strategy for the personal action plan. For example, your marketing plan may tell you that you need to find and create three professional strategic alliances with professionals who share your target market but do not compete with your services. You may want to enact this strategy by the end of the quarter.

> "A marketing plan is a strategy that outlines what you will do, with whom, and when you will take action."

Then, your personal action plan will break down into chunks every item that needs to happen in order to accomplish that. For example, it can run the gamut of researching three appropriate partners, creating a draft email you could send to each, thinking of two creative ways in which you could support them, thinking of one way in which you want to ask them to support you, updating your bio, creating a one-page flyer that speaks to what you do, and putting three dates in your calendar to ask each potential partner if they would like to meet to discuss the benefits of alignment.

Why You Need a Marketing Plan First

The objective of a good marketing plan is to get yourself in the right place with the right people at the right time in the right headset so that you can have a perfect exchange. You can accomplish that only by doing your homework first—that is, by logging the "brain pushups" or marketing strategizing—so that once you meet your ideal client you're certain to have everything you need to have an energizing exchange that leaves him or her feeling attracted to working with you. You want to inspire the thinking in that prospective client of "Wow! I want to be around that person."

Of course, you must be in the presence of a potential new client in order to demonstrate your value, so being where potential clients are is the first and most important step to guaranteeing your continued livelihood. The following marketing methods can provide you with opportunities to interact directly with your potential audience—in person, on the phone, or online. Experience tells me that these particular methods are remarkably effective for coaches (in no particular order):

- writing (articles, books, blogs, e-zines, etc.)
- speaking (keynotes, conference break-outs, workshops, seminars, etc.)
- creating and maintaining a casual "let's keep-in-touch" strategy (birthday cards, LinkedIn, newsletter, e-zines, postcards, sending articles from the newspaper if you see relevance to your target with a cover note initiating a real dialogue)
- asking clients for referrals
- networking (at symposiums, trade shows, industry events)
- creating strategic alliances (with a few professionals).

Which of these methods interests you? Although a multi-touch approach is highly recommended and typically the most successful, nothing says you have to use every single method for your practice. I strongly suggest that you put your energy toward only those things you are happy to do.

Marketing doesn't have to be doing work you fear or dislike; it is and can be about doing work you love, building on strengths, and bringing in support when and where you need it. So, if you dread writing, that's okay, pick two or three other strategies that appeal to you. If you don't like it, don't do it. It will never work if you hate it and the gremlins will say " I told you so," reinforcing the old hardwired and misguided belief system ingrained many moons ago that you are not a good marketer. Phooey!

Strategic Alliances

For those times that you can't be directly in front of the client, a strategic alliance can be helpful. A *strategic alliance* is composed of two highly committed professionals who share some or all of a targeted market profile. If you are in a strategic alliance, your partner's service will not overlap with yours. Instead, he or she will be a potential referral partner (and vice versa). The two of you will share the same target market without competing with each other.

> "A strategic alliance is a powerful way to build your business and expand your marketing capacity beyond your normal reach."

For example, one of my target markets is entrepreneurial female leaders. My bookkeeper specializes in helping small, woman-owned businesses manage their books. We thus share a similar target market. Interestingly enough, my doctor owns and operates a number of women's health services practices, so we too have an overlap in our target market. As such, my doctor knows many women whom she gives my card to for leadership coaching. Both my bookkeeper and doctor are ripe resources for referrals for me when it comes to female entrepreneurial leaders, as I am for them.

The idea is that your strategic partner's clients and prospects are clients you want as well. Aligning can help you both attract more attention to what it is that you create. This often results in more clients for each.

A strategic alliance therefore is a win–win relationship in which decision-making is shared between the partners, and strategic goals are achieved together that could not be achieved alone. The whole equals more than the sum of its parts.

Tips for creating an effective alliance include:

- make your partner's success your top priority
- educate your partner about coaching and help him or her fall in love with what you do
- ask them to outline how you can help them fill their practice (how many referrals they would like each month and how they would like to receive them?)
- outline how your partner can help you fill your practice (how many referrals would you like each month and how would you like to receive them?)
- communicate every month with your partner about how you're doing with helping him or her
- thank your partner genuinely, often, and, if you can, publicly, on your blog, in your newsletter, etc.
- always ask your partner what you can be doing better for him or her.

When looking to create a *professional coaching strategic alliance*, you can draw from a number of sources. These might include community leaders, talent managers, human resource consultants, church leaders, bankers, lawyers, teachers, president of clubs, doctors, organizational development professionals, and professors of graduate schools.

Sources for *personal coaching strategic alliances* might include community leaders, personal trainers, gym owners, salon owners, chiropractors, nutritionists, financial advisors, and healing professionals.

All of these are possible referral partners to you as long as you share the same type of client without offering the same services or competing with each other. Once again, the idea is that these people's client lists are full of your future clients. In teaming up, you both help each other spread the word and refer your clients to each other.

Sample Alliance Strategy

A strategic alliance is a powerful way to build your business and expand your marketing capacity beyond your normal reach. To build your own strategic alliances, I recommend the following approach:

1. Make a list of at least two potential strategic alliance prospects.
2. Find out who the key decision makers are at each organization and get their coordinates.
3. Ask them for a meeting where you learn the following: What are your members' key concerns right now? What are the hot topics they want to learn about? How can I add value to your members in addition to what you offer? If I were able to add value in this way, what difference would it make to you and to your members?
4. Invite them to create an alliance with you: "How might we join forces to create more value for our target markets?"

Creating an alliance with a partner requires establishing trust, sharing common objectives, and making a commitment to a plan that you both hold each other accountable to.

KEY INSIGHTS

- *A marketing plan is a strategy or blueprint for what you will do, with whom, and by when in order to build your client base.*

- *There are several marketing strategies at your disposal; implementing the three most suited to your personality will keep you energized and engaged in the marketing process.*

- *A strategic alliance is one of the fastest and most effective ways to create a full practice.*

Classroom Exercises

Exercise 21-A: Marketing Plan

Target Client Group 1: How do you reach this target audience? How will you come to have your target audience experience you?

Strategies:

1.

2.

3.

Target Client Group 2: How do you reach them? How will you come to have them experience you?

Strategies:

1.

2.

3.

Target Client Group 3: How do you reach them? How will you come to have them experience you?

Strategies:

1.

2.

3.

Exercise 21-B: Strategic Alliances

Identify three people who can provide you with exactly what you need to expand your network and fill your practice.

1.

2.

3.

Exercise 21-C: Strategic Alliance Exercises

How could you work something out with your strategic partner that would benefit everyone involved and help you both attract new clients? What types of initiatives can you conduct with a strategic partner, as a team?

Name three things can you team up with a strategic partner to do.

1.

2.

3.

Resources

Marketing Plan Template (see Appendix L)

Find Your Natural Marketing Style (see Appendix M)

Fieldwork

Finish the marketing plan for one target market using the template in Appendix L.

In addition, finish the previous Classroom Exercise.

OBJECTIVES

Identify and start creating the materials you will need to put your top three marketing strategies into action

MODULE 22: *What Tools Do You Need?*

At Your Disposal: A Look at Your Marketing Tools

Marketing tools run the gamut from a brochure to a headshot. Essentially, these are aids to help you feel confident and prepared to approach your target market.

Which marketing tools will you need? Here is a sample list, compiled from my coaching students:

- business card
- bio
- letter of introduction
- one-pager
- newsletter
- website
- blog
- testimonials (see Appendix N for ideas on how to collect these)
- client contract and forms
- wardrobe

- headshot
- printer, fax, PC

Let's look at how some of these tools can be used to enact various marketing strategies:

- business card – hand out at industry networking events after good conversations
- bio – email your bio to several local and regional moms groups with an offer to do a free back-to-work seminar
- letter of introduction – mail to college career offices, with an offer to provide free coaching hours once a month
- newsletter – send once a month to individuals you've met at industry networking events to share client-success stories and special offers.

Typically, you will need several marketing tools in order to enact each of your strategies (note how in the previous example both business cards *and* newsletters were given to industry leads—and this would just be the tip of the iceberg). Using multiple marketing tools will allow you to build trust and credibility with a potential client over time. We know from Sherven and Sniechowski's *The Heart of Marketing* that clients need to be exposed to you several times before they feel comfortable buying from you, right?

Also important, some tools are better suited for certain marketing strategies than others. For example, you may have a colorful, creative

> "Using multiple marketing tools will allow you to build trust and credibility with a potential client over time."

business card and an irreverent blog that work great for attracting your musician and artist clients, but for the segment of your practice directed at attracting traditional corporate clients, you find that classic business cards and a straightforward print newsletter work better. Determining the right tool for the right strategy—and prioritizing these strategies and tools along the way—will help you get the most out of your marketing efforts.

What are the ways in which you will reach your target audience?

KEY INSIGHTS

- *You will need to create several marketing tools to enact each of your strategies.*

- *It is important to identify which tools are needed for which strategy and to prioritize their creation.*

Classroom Exercises

Make a list of the tools you will need in order to enact your top three marketing strategies.

_____

_____

_____

_____

_____

_____

_____

_____

_____

_____

_____

_____

Resources

Marketing Plan Template (see Appendix L)

Fieldwork

Refine your list of tools and prioritize which you will need first and by when.

OBJECTIVES

Develop a personal action plan to execute your marketing strategies and to ensure that you create the coaching practice that you intend

MODULE 23: *Building Your Personal Action Plan*

Background

Action planning is a process that will help you decide what steps you need to take to achieve each of your marketing strategies (identified in Module 21). Your *personal action plan* is a statement of what you want to achieve over a given period of time. Preparing an action plan is an effective way to help you to reach your marketing objectives.

Your personal action plan is a document that you will create and refine over time. It is a map of what you will do by when, what issues you might face, and the resources you will rely upon for strength and support. At its base, your personal action plan is a logical, sequential outline of steps that when taken, one at a time, get you closer to your goal of building a profitable and sustainable coaching practice.

Having a map eliminates the "what if's" and "how will I ever's" that threaten to undermine you. It helps you manage the inner critic, who tends to run rampant when you don't have a concrete visualization for how you will get from here to there. The best way to stop worrying is to start planning!

For example, if I have to drive to a new place in an area I am unfamiliar with, I not only research the directions on the Internet, but I also use my car's global positioning system. This way, I don't have to worry about getting lost, being late, and ultimately disappointing myself and others who may be waiting for me. A map helps you get where you're going with greater mental and physical ease.

Your personal action plan is just like a travel map in that you consistently refer to it to keep yourself headed in the right direction. If you get off course, you know it and can self-correct. I like to keep mine on my corkboard so I can see it every day. I also have it as a handy icon on my computer desktop so I can edit it daily. It is a fluid document that will change as you move through the steps you have planned.

> "Your personal action plan is a logical, sequential outline of steps that, when taken, get you closer to your goal of building a profitable and sustainable coaching practice."

Earlier, we said that successful entrepreneurs are aware of how they think and are focused on how to improve how they think. They also create written action plans that they hold themselves accountable to, and they edit those plans continually.

Creating your personal action plan may seem daunting when you're starting out because there is simply so much to do, but once you create the first 3 to 6 steps, you can see it for what it really is—a simple plan of action, a to-do list. For a beginner, that list may sound rudimentary—write my bio, select a company name, create a design for my business card, and choose a web designer. But we don't want to confuse rudimentary with straightforward or straightforward with unimportant. Make no mistake. Each of these actions is an important part of your larger plan because it comes together to create your overall company, brand, and impact.

To create your personal action plan, you will want to create a simple document or spreadsheet, whatever works best for you (see Appendix O for one sample). In that document or spreadsheet, plan to address the following areas.

Specific Actions You Will Take. The heart of your personal action plan will consist of the to-do items you need to complete to accomplish your marketing strategy. You can start creating your plan by listing out all the things you need to do to enact the first marketing strategy that you outlined for yourself in your Marketing Plan, created in Module 21. The simplest way to start is to break down your marketing strategy into doable action steps. Then, once you have listed all of the steps, you can prioritize them. What has to be done first to allow for later to-do items to follow?

Let's explore what some of these action steps might look like. If one of your target markets is baby boomers preparing for retirement and your first marketing strategy to connect to this group involves meeting these potential clients at retirement-planning conventions, you would begin creating your personal action plan by listing out the to-do items necessary to get to these conventions and meet your clients there. Your to-do list might look something like this:

- search online for the most popular retirement-planning conventions in the United States and select five to seven for possible attendance
- create a spreadsheet comparing costs to travel to, exhibit, and advertise at each convention
- call each conference planner to learn more about the event, assess its potential, and investigate opportunities to provide free seminars
- interview five baby boomers who have previously attended one of these conferences and ask them what they enjoyed most, wish had

been different, and would like to see more of at the conference.

- And so on...

When you chunk a big strategy down into baby steps, you have, in effect, crafted a specific, tactical to-do list for yourself. It's easier to take small steps toward a big goal than to try to run a whole marathon the first time you're out jogging. Small steps over time add up to great accomplishment.

Assign a Due Date for Each Action. It's vitally important to include the targeted due date for each action item so that you know where you are at any given time, relative to your plan. Using the earlier baby boomer market example, you might assign a due date of three days from now to complete your online research for retirement conventions, one week from now to have created your spreadsheet, two weeks from now to have spoken to all of the convention planners, and four weeks from now to have spoken to past conference attendees. Each of these action items would have a specific due date that you would then mark on your planning calendar, for example, March 1, March 7, March 14, and April 1. By specifying dates, you create a sense of urgency for each item, while helping to prioritize which items need to be completed first. Over time, you can adjust, refine, and expand your personal action plan as needed.

In your personal action plan, you will also note what obstacles you might face and the resources you will rely upon for strength and support. Planning for these areas will help you keep moving forward and stay accountable to your plan even when challenges pop up. We will discuss these areas of the personal action plan in the next module.

The personal action plan is one of the essential keys to creating success in your coaching practice as it moves you from thinking to doing and empowers you to translate your strategy into real-world success.

KEY INSIGHTS

- *Your personal action plan is a map of what you will do by when, what issues you might face, and the resources you will rely upon for strength and support when enacting your marketing strategies.*

- *Each to-do item in your personal action plan, no matter how small or "simple," is an important part of your plan because it integrates with the other action steps to create your overall company, brand, and impact.*

Classroom Exercises

Let's start to create your personal action plan, using the template in Appendix O and making sure to cite specific actions and due dates for each action.

Resources

Your Personal Action Plan (see Appendix O)

Fieldwork

Continue to create and then polish your personal action plan.

OBJECTIVES

Understand the role of support and accountability in creating your success

MODULE 24: *Leveraging Accountability to Create Success*

Background

Over the past six years, I have seen many coaches fail, whether due to fear, lack of business knowledge, lack of coaching competence, or lack of support, accountability, and follow-through. Each of these issues can be addressed in their own right (e.g., through sufficient training, continuing education classes, mentorship, etc.). In this module, we will help you hedge against failure due to a lack of accountability by exploring its importance and designing a plan for accountability in your personal action plan.

Impact of Accountability

Have you ever seen a successful entrepreneur and wondered how he or she achieved so much? There are many elements and secrets to entrepreneurial success, but let's focus on this one: Most successful entrepreneurs have a coach. Consider these statistics from the American Society of Training and Development, which reveal the probability of successfully completing a goal:

- 10% if you hear an idea
- 25% if you consciously decide to adopt it
- 40% if you decide when you will do it
- 50% if you plan how you will do it
- 65% if you commit to someone else you will do it
- 95% if you have a specific accountability appointment with the person to whom you committed.

If these statistics don't demonstrate the value of having a coach, I'm not sure what does! Being a coach yourself, you are likely to see the value of having a specific accountability partner and scheduled meetings to check in, brainstorm, and explore. Right? Or do you think that you don't need a coach because you are one? Now, I'm sure that you know what I'm going to say about that...

Everyone needs a powerful coach! It's amazing to see how much faster you grow when led by a coach or a marketing mentor. The benefit from aligning with a coach is the new perspectives they offer. Equally important are the resources, accountability, and encouragement that a coach provides, ensuring that you stay the course and reach your desired outcome, supporting you with what it takes to thrive. When you're accountable to someone, it increases the likelihood that you'll achieve your goals.

> "When you're accountable to someone, it increases the likelihood that you'll achieve your goals."

Don't forget about mastermind groups, either. It helps tremendously to be supported and held accountable by a powerful group of like-minded people who believe in your potential. You can do anything with that level of energy and support.

So I want you to resist all the common coaching objections like "I can't justify the cost!" and "I don't have time." I say, "Oh, yes you can" and "Yes, you do." How can you afford not to? If you invest in coaching now, you will see the dividends in your thriving practice later.

Adding Accountability Into the Personal Action Plan

We learned in previous modules that developing a marketing plan (a marketing strategy that outlines what you will do, with whom, and when) will help guide you toward your meaningful and successful practice. Until you take that action, though, your objectives have no chance of being realized. It's support and accountability that will help you move from planning to action—so let's jump in and add those pieces to your personal action plan.

Obstacles You Might Encounter. Think now about what might get in the way of taking your stated actions. Money? Access? Time? What could block or challenge you? What could get in the way? Anticipating your obstacles paves the way for working through them.

Tactics for Overcoming Obstacles. After laying out which potential obstacles you may face, you will be better equipped to develop tactics for dealing with those obstacles. What will you specifically do, who will you call upon, and how will you redirect yourself if you find yourself facing any of these obstacles? Developing a plan for overcoming obstacles lessens the chance you will get waylaid or side-railed on your mission to build and market your coaching practice.

How Will You Hold Yourself Accountable and Keep Yourself Moving Forward? The best way to ensure that goals get completed is to set up accountability—a mechanism through which you have to answer for whether or not you've completed action items. What strategies will you use to make sure you complete your action items? How will you stay energized and motivated to complete your action items? It could be software or social-media tools that help you keep track of and share the status and health of your goals, weekly planning sessions—or nightly journaling. You get to experiment and discover which techniques work best for you.

What Resources Can You Call Upon for Help? In light of the earlier statistics, the power of working with someone else to stay accountable can't really be denied. What type of support works best for you? A coach buddy, a marketing mentor, or someone else? Set up your support system *before* you need it. Let's face it—when we need support, we are usually too blocked to create it.

By building accountability into your personal action plan, you make sure that all of your planning does not go to waste. A coach, mastermind group, or accountability buddy will give you that boost you need to move from plan into action. They can help you get motivated, troubleshoot problems, and stay on track. This kind of support will accelerate the process of achieving your dream practice because your efforts will not be made in a vacuum but within a community of people cheering on your success.

You have worked hard to get to this point. Now, it's time to manifest results.

KEY INSIGHTS

- When you're accountable to someone, it *greatly* increases the likelihood you'll achieve your goals.

- Accountability is a strong reason why coaching works.

- Coaches need coaches, mentors, support, and accountability too!

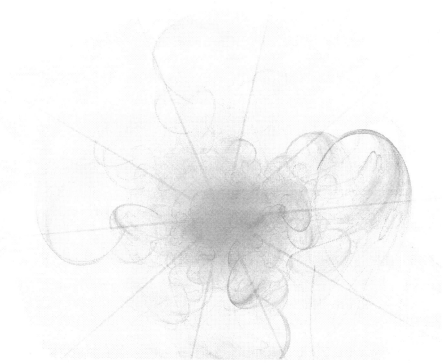

Classroom Exercises

Obstacles I might encounter:

_____

_____

_____

Tactics for overcoming obstacles:

_____

_____

_____

How do I hold myself accountable and keep myself moving forward?

_____

_____

_____

What resources can I call upon for help?

_____

_____

_____

Fieldwork

For homework, please complete the rest of your action plan (see Appendix L).

Also connect with a classmate/partner to whom you will stay accountable on your personal action plan now and in the future.

OBJECTIVES

Learn, through practice,
how to naturally deliver your
marketing messages

MODULE 25: *Marketing Laboratory*

Background

Let's practice!

You will be thrown curveball questions from time to time. The best way to prepare for them is to practice staying present when they are hurled. Let's look at a list of the questions or remarks that may make you want to run for cover, and, then, let's practice responding to them in class, in the safety of pairs.

Classroom Exercises

- You are at a party where an academic associate of the host asks you to clarify the methodology behind coaching. What do you say?

- At a dinner party, a guest suggests that as a coach you are playing with people's lives.

- A family member is adamant that you need a psychology degree or counseling qualification in order to help people work though their obstacles. How do you respond?

- A prospective client challenges you by saying, "Coaching is for people with problems." How do you respond?

- You are challenged by a colleague who says that coaching is the latest fad in self-development and it won't last. What do you say?

Fieldwork

Find a fellow coach to practice with and ask the other person the question—or say the remark—that most makes him or her uncomfortable. One question each way.

OBJECTIVES

*Summarize what
you have learned*

*Answer any
remaining questions*

*Ensure that you connect to a
classmate/partner
for accountability*

*Complete your learning journey
in a way that supports you
to move forward armed
with confidence and ease*

MODULE 26: *Learning Debrief*

Background

My hope in this book (and class) has been to turn your understanding of marketing on its head. While most of us think that marketing is just the act of doing—talking about our services, writing about our services, and giving samples of our services (and that is certainly part of the picture)—we can never forget that, first, marketing is *being*. Effective marketing—and the kind of marketing that I know you cannot just live with but enjoy—begins with being true to who you are. It's not about talking the sales talk or walking the sales walk; it's about literally living out loud the passion you feel for your work so that others are drawn to you and what it is that you do. They see your value and want to capture a piece of it for themselves.

Conscious Marketing is defined as authentically and naturally revealing who you are and what you offer, so as to attract and engage the people you most want to work with. It's re-engaging with your contribution and speaking from that place of understanding to let people know about what you do in your life's work and how you can help clients. Conscious Marketing is about staying aware of what you are thinking and doing and why and using your positive thoughts to consciously shape your marketing outcomes. Conscious Marketing isn't about selling your services; it's about sharing your passion and making clear how you turn that passion into value for the client.

It's time to unleash the power of your thoughts. It's time to capture your favorite clients. It's time to do what you love and to love telling people about what you do. It's time to consciously market.

Your dream coaching practice is waiting...

Classroom Exercises

What will you have to do to make marketing an authentic extension of who you are?

_____

_____

_____

_____

Share your top three insights about what it is going to take for you to stay present when you speak about the services you provide.

_____

_____

_____

_____

What do you now know about marketing that you did not know on day one?

_____

_____

_____

_____

What do you now see about marketing yourself that will allow you to move forward with more comfort?

_____

_____

_____

_____

Resources

Marketing Plan Template (see Appendix L)

Your Personal Action Plan (see Appendix O)

Fieldwork

This assignment is due to the instructor via email by midnight the day after class ends.

1. Polish up and refine your targeted marketing plan for one target market.

2. Look again at the action plan started in class. Complete it. Identify the first three action steps you will take and indicate by when.

3. Answer the following question in approximately 200 words: What is it going to specifically take for you to market yourself powerfully, authentically, and with confidence once you leave this classroom?

APPENDIX A

Conscious Marketing Assessment

This assessment will help you get clear about what you currently think, feel, and do in relation to marketing and about the results this has created. It will also help you get present to what you want instead. It positions you to build a plan to fill the gap.

Taking this inventory will help you decide whether you need a dose of Conscious Marketing to close your gap. Each area of the assessment addresses a facet of marketing where you can create new thinking and, hence, take better, smarter, and more action on your part.

Instructions:

Rate yourself from 0 to 5 for each statement in the Conscious Marketing assessment below. (If you prefer, you may take the assessment online, print the results, and bring them to class; see www.consciouscoachinginstitute. com/assess/). Note that *0* indicates no confidence in an area and *5* indicates a high level of comfort or strength in the area. At the end of the assessment, follow the instructions to help you focus in on where you're starting your personal journey to Conscious Marketing.

My Thinking, Being, and Feeling About Marketing

Purpose and Vision: I can articulate to my clients what my purpose is and what my vision is for them. I live it and it is inherent in all my materials. _____

Presence: I am congruent with my purpose and vision for clients and my practice. I am deeply present to them as I take action. I know what I am doing and why. _____

Agenda: When I speak to a potential client about their needs, I am clearly focused on the value I can provide for *them*—not about making a sale. _____

Fear, Doubt, Worry: I notice my fear, doubt and worry gremlins. I know their scripts. By noticing them, I'm then able to put them aside and consciously create new thinking. _____

Belief Systems: I am aware of my negative thoughts and feelings around marketing: what marketing is, how it feels, and my competency and comfort with it. I see where these beliefs sabotage me.

_____

New Mental Models: I know I can create a new mental model of marketing that serves me, one that feels organic and natural by changing my thoughts. _____

Establishing Trust: I gain trust and establish intimacy such that the prospect opens up in a way that an honest, open dialogue can occur. I understand what trust behaviors look like and demonstrate them naturally. _____

Confidence: When I talk about what I do and the results I create, I neither play big nor small. I am grounded in "what is." _____

Professionalism: My systems, services and procedures are tight. _____

Congruence: My words, way with people, and materials are fully integrated and clearly communicate who I am. _____

Authenticity: Everything, including my personal image and materials, authentically communicates who I am. _____

Signature Style: I am fully expressed. This means I have my signature stamp on my work. Anyone picking up my card, brochure, etc., would know it's me without seeing my name. I have a brand. _____

Doing: Creating My Messages

Target: I have identified who my targeted audience is—those with whom I feel the most self-expressed and energized about working with. _____

Problems: I have identified what problems, pain, and challenges this segment faces. _____

Solutions: I have identified the solutions that correlate to the problems they face. _____

Core Statement: I have a well thought out, ten-second statement that conveys who my ideal client is, their problems, and what solutions I bring to bear. _____

Value: I can articulate several benefits that my clients will experience when they follow through with my solution. _____

Differentiation: I know what sets me apart from other coaches and why a client should choose me. I can state this succinctly. _____

My Story: I can naturally and succinctly talk about my background, experience, and what a client can expect from me. _____

Client-Success Stories: I have three written, well rehearsed client success stories at my mental fingertips to share about a similar problem that I solved. _____

Credibility: I can clearly and confidently state why I am qualified to deliver on my promises without feeling awkward. _____

Doing: My Conversational Skills

Direct Communication: I am clear that the key to engaging and acquiring clients is clear and authentic communication. I am regularly honoring these skills. _____

Powerful Questions: I have an arsenal of specific questions aimed at uncovering the client's pain or goal, level of commitment to change, and readiness to say yes to me. _____

Listening for Potential: I listen for my client's potential as I communicate my ability to facilitate solutions. I stand for the future objectives they want to accomplish even when I am marketing. _____

Doing: My Strategy and Blueprint

Referrals: I have multiple ways to gain referrals from existing clients. Referrals are my number one source for new clients. _____

Networking: I am in front of my target markets by attending social and business events that allow for face-to-face interaction and exposure. _____

Speaking: I share my expertise by speaking—be it seminars, workshops, lectures, or key note speeches. _____

Writing: I enjoy writing about what I do and have something valuable to share. _____

Alliances: I know three professionals with non-competing services that are committed to providing me with referrals and vice versa. _____

Offers: I have several offers to make so that my conversation with a prospect need not come to a halt. I provide them with no-cost opportunities to experience more of me. _____

Constant Touch: I consistently communicate with prospects and clients by sharing useful and relevant information. _____

Plan: I have a simple, thorough plan for each target market that outlines what I will do and when, and what tools are needed. _____

Doing: My Personal Action Plans for Success

Marketing Messages and Plans: I am enrolled in a program where I am getting clear about who I am as a coach, what I do and for whom, my messages, and my strategic plan to make it all happen authentically. _____

Accountability: I am an active member of a marketing mastermind group composed of entrepreneurial coaches to keep me inspired, fresh, and on task. _____

Mentoring: I work with a mentor coach who has a successful coaching business and whose approach resonates for me. _____

APPENDIX B

Conscious Marketing Model

Core Messages

My Story

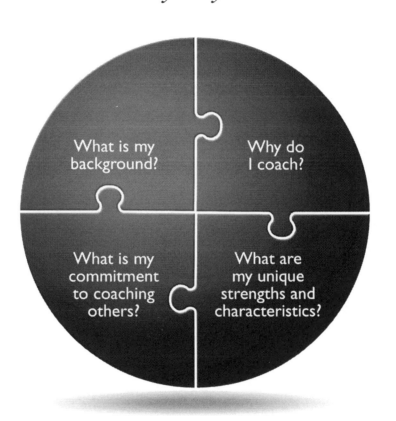

My Client Offers

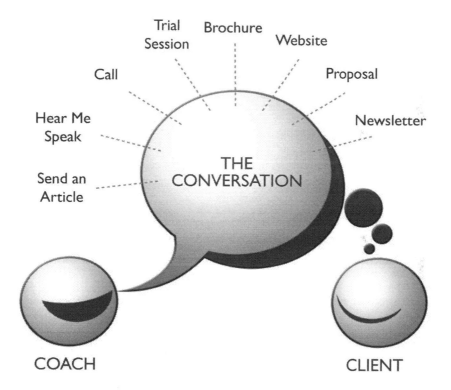

Client Story

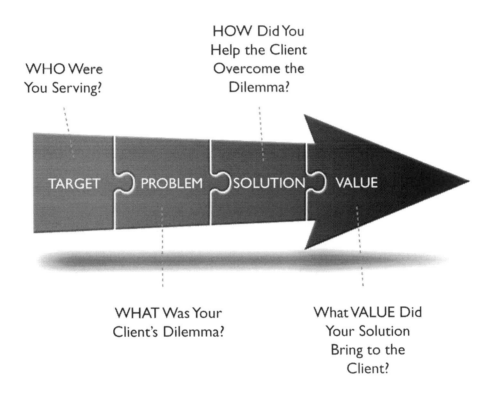

APPENDIX C

Sample Turnaround Statements for Self-Limiting Beliefs

Marketing

I'm not a salesperson and don't want to sell. I don't relate to pushy sales-people and don't want to be perceived that way.

> → *I choose to be natural and unassuming when talking to people about what I do.*

I don't have a background in marketing so I don't know what I'm doing.

> → *I choose to use my experience as a leader, entrepreneur, executive, and woman to drive my marketing plan.*

I don't trust marketing. I'm always looking for the catch. It sounds too good to be true. I value honesty and don't want to do anything that would make someone suspicious. Spinning something is as bad as being dishonest.

> → *I choose to be real and honest in my marketing approach and give clients more return on their investment than they expected.*

227

My natural tendency is to be shy, so it is difficult for me to network and talk about myself.

> → *I choose to use my natural curiosity and love of helping people to connect with others.*

Money

People won't be able to afford my fees.

> → *I choose to let others determine their finances.*

My fee is the same or higher than people in other helping professions and I have less education.

> → *I choose to give my clients the highest value for their investment.*

I moved to a small community where people don't expect to pay a lot.

> → *I choose to believe that people will pay for something that has value to them.*

Being an Entrepreneur

I'm not creative enough to come up with something brand new and fresh.

> → *I choose to use my creativity to enhance my company's offerings.*

You have to be really smart about a lot of things in order to be successful as an entrepreneur. I don't have the expertise in many of the areas needed to be successful.

> → *I choose to embrace all of my new learning and have fun experimenting.*

Who is she to coach me? I had a higher position than she did.

> → *I choose to offer exceptional value to my clients.*

APPENDIX D

Student Samples to Inspire New Mental Models

Talk about a time when you connected with someone and felt natural and comfortable in speaking about what you do.

> "When I looked at the times that I've connected with people, it's when I didn't view the interaction as selling; it's when I was honest, straightforward, and sincerely wanted to help the other person. My motivation was not what I would get in return but rather what I would be able to do for that person. This was true whether I was coaching one of my employees as part of their development or communicating a difficult message to a group. My team trusted me and I realized that I place a very high importance on this value."

A Student's Current Mental Model of Marketing

> "Some marketing is a form of manipulation such as buying a car. I've had the experience of a salesperson wearing me down and taking advantage of my fatigue to sell me a vehicle. I felt used and

abused. I'm pretty distrustful of salespeople and so I'm typically on the defense about what's in it for them.

For that reason, I self-invest all of my money and only utilize a fee-for-service financial planner who gets no commission for his investment recommendations. I'm curious but cautious when buying. Good salespeople find out what I need and offer products that are suitable.

When I have to sell myself, I typically feel awkward and believe that others are as skeptical as I am. I probably don't find out enough about their needs before giving them a spiel and I certainly don't feel natural and authentic."

A Student's New Mental Model of Marketing

"In my mental movie, people gravitate to me because of my energy and are naturally curious about what I do. Roll the tapes: I move and speak with natural confidence and warmth. I greet every person who is naturally put in my path or with whom I feel a pull toward. I smile, make eye contact, and say something that feels natural. Maybe I will simply extend my hand to introduce myself and ask them their name in return or, perhaps, seeing them will spark a thought that I feel compelled to share.

Perhaps, I have been enjoying their presence or I have a question and decide that they are the one I want to ask. I take it as it comes. I let it happen. When I am centered, the words flow effortlessly.

My energy field feels like a cozy rest stop. They feel they can let their guard down with me and this surprises them because they just met me. They enjoy the fun of feeling close quickly and decide to take another risk by asking me curious, somewhat personal, questions, which I answer honestly and candidly. This allows for us to quickly engage in a meaningful dialogue around sharing who we are. I then decide to ask them a few powerful, visioning questions and listen intently and actively as they speak.

We allow the conversation to take us where it leads and we are both feeling fully present. We forget to mingle with others and feel a little self-conscious about that. After some time, we both share that we enjoyed our time together chatting and look forward to speaking again soon.

Then, we agree to exchange numbers. They call me in a few days and ask if they can learn more about coaching with me. They thank me for agreeing to help them and they look forward to getting started."

What do you now see about marketing yourself that will allow you to move forward with more comfort and ease? How does this new learning connect with what you've seen about how you used to think, feel, and act with respect to marketing?

"I registered for this course in spite of great discomfort around choosing to coach professionally. I didn't see the need to market myself, and yet I was unable to verbalize what it was I intended to accomplish. By the end of our first class, I saw how resistant I have been to identifying my top target market, my niche, and my core message. Living in that world has been totally disempowering and unfulfilling—I haven't been able to verbalize what I do!

The class exercises 'calmed' me down considerably. For the first time, I saw my top target market clearly and [saw] that I possess the tools

I need to focus on that market. I have lived it after all! After class, it was a joy to *want* to put pen to paper. Marketing myself is now occurring to me as essential, and not a 'nice-to-have but not-for-me' tool. Identifying my top target market is not confining, but actually liberating. I am empowered to share my unique abilities with my audience. I see a clear roadmap of who my audience is, the problems that confront them, and the solutions that I can offer them."

How I need to look at marketing in order to be successful, natural, and abundant.

- Marketing is a process of determining someone's needs and matching what I have to offer to fulfill those needs.
- I need to be confident that I am giving people significant value and return on their investment.
- I need to be honest and straightforward.
- I need to offer a free trial so people can experience coaching first hand and determine whether it's for them.
- I need to ask for referrals once people have experienced coaching first hand.
- I need to build relationships first!
- I need to ask questions to get to know the person before I tell them what I do.
- I need to make my marketing conversational, natural, and authentic.
- My love for what I do has to shine through.

APPENDIX E

Additional Questions for Guided Vision

What specialized knowledge do you have to bring to bear?

- Take quick stock of your experiences in and outside of coaching.
- What sources of uniqueness do you have?
- What expertise do you have that you could add to this picture?
- What else do you have passion about that you could add to this mix?

What is the value you provide in the role you envision for yourself?

- What is it that you are really providing?
- What does that mean to you?
- Why does it matter to you?
- Is there a theme?

Who are you working with?

- Who are the most exciting groups you can see yourself working with as clients?
- What excites you about them?
- Who else do you daydream about working with?
- What qualities or areas of focus do they have, and why do they excite you?

What are you getting out of it?

- How do you benefit from working with these groups?
- How do you feel after working with them?
- What's your level of motivation to work with them?

What are the benefits to others of providing this service?

- What are *they* getting out it?
- What are the best things you do for them?

What problems do the client groups you are working with have?

- What do they struggle with?
- What's in the front of their minds?
- What keeps them feeling stuck?
- What do they worry about?

How do you know you provide the value and benefits that you do?

- Why are you qualified to do this?
- What results have you produced for others?
- Can you think of a time when you did this for someone?
- What is relevant about that story?

How do you imagine your paths crossing with them?

- Where do they hang out, eat, play, work, and learn?
- How do you imagine a conversation happening where you discover there is a match between what they're looking for and what you provide?
- What tools do you see yourself communicating with?
- What characteristics or qualities do those tools have?

What qualities do you see that you and your work embody?

- What is unique and special about you and how you work?

APPENDIX F

Sample Target Market Exercise

Sample Exercise #1

Target: Creative Professionals

Age Range: 25-65

Gender: Male or female

Level of Education: College graduate

Geographical Location: International

Annual Income Level: $100,000 plus

Professions: Creative Professionals, Executives, and Leaders, esp. Fashion Designer, Creative Director, Trend Forecaster, Art Director, Film Director, Costume Designer, Cinematographer

Industries: Fashion, Trend Forecasting, Beauty, Fragrance, Interior Design, Advertising, Film, Theatre

Job Title or Position: Owner, CEO, Creative Director, EVP/SVP/VP of Design, High Potentials

Psychological Needs:

- Must be actively engaged with their environment
- Must be creatively satisfied and stimulated and likes to be hungry for more
- Searching for a sense of security and greater achievement
- Experiencing a fragile sense of self-worth
- Lacking connectedness with their work/life balance and what drives them to succeed
- No longer feeling they are a source of contribution
- Looking for a richer, more fulfilling life
- At a crossroads
- At worst, may be feeling creatively and spiritually bankrupt

Personal Interests:

- A satisfying romantic relationship
- Earning money
- A search for spiritual peace
- Art and design, film, theater
- Travel, exotic cultures
- Luxury

When do they buy what you're selling? When...

- They are having difficulty maintaining a work and life balance
- They are not feeling creatively fulfilled
- They are searching for a meaningful intimate or romantic relationship
- They are feeling disillusioned and empty

How do they buy your services?

- Word-of-mouth (I am known to cause breakthroughs in performance and actions).
- I have a blog.
- I have a website.
- They discover me at networking functions (e.g., Fashion Group and the Council of Fashion Designers of America).
- I am a keynote speaker.
- I have a television show.

What do they perceive they are buying?

- A generous listener.
- Access to a coach who understands the value of work and life balance.
- I am a single mother of a thriving 19-year-old.
- Access to realizing the life of their dreams.
- Working with a master at transformational coaching. I have lived and experienced what they are going through and have caused personal and professional breakthroughs for myself and others.
- Access to working with an experienced, award-winning leader and creative in the fashion industry (20+ years, i.e., I have been the CEO of my own fashion brand for 8 years and I have 12 years' experience managing the design studio for two 1-billion-dollar retail brands).

What other types of professional services do they buy?

- Career Coaching
- Therapist
- Personal Trainers
- Internet Dating
- Massage Therapist

- Astrologer
- Professional Organizer
- Personal Shopper
- Nutritionist
- Esthetician

Who do they have regular contact with?

- Primarily their work community, followed by their friends and family

Who are they likely to turn to when making a difficult decision?

- They tend to make difficult decisions on their own, though they may also speak to a family member or close friend. They may have a therapist as well.

What kinds of people or businesses do they trust?

- They trust people with proven track records and tangible results. Regarding their personal life, this could mean someone who "came through" for them when they needed them most.
- They trust their therapist, if they have one.

Preferred style of communication (email, phone, or in person)?

- My client prefers to have an in-person session but often relies on phone calls due to time constraints. The client is also comfortable with email.

Sample Exercise #2

Entrepreneurs, leaders, coaches, and ascending female leaders aged 20–60

Recognize that they need a strong thinking partner

Are willing to work hard, be accountable, be vulnerable, and stay open

Don't negotiate about price

Respect time—both mine and theirs

Are honest, bright, and ready

Choose to face and conquer challenges before them

Don't let fear stop them

Profusely thank me for helping them make change

Get such good results that they rave about me and refer me to their colleagues

APPENDIX G

Sample List of Solutions

Interpersonal Competencies Solutions for Executives

- Gain knowledge and insight into themselves and the organization, which allows executives to become more flexible and versatile
- Acknowledge and understand feelings and apply them more effectively in the workplace to improve and develop working relationships
- Work through blockages and resistance to change
- Recognize where previous strengths (e.g., an independent, autonomous style) have become a liability (e.g., in teamwork)
- Recognize and effectively manage stress
- Deal with conflict, both personal and with colleagues
- Modify interpersonal style, such as moving from a competitive to a more collaborative stance
- Develop trusting relationships with clients and colleagues
- Develop advanced communication skills, such as maximize verbal and non-verbal interactions, listen, give feedback (especially praise), and understand, predict, and alter patterns of communication

Skill Development Solutions for Executives

- Learn and improve leadership skills—recognize and develop leadership competencies, for example, increase awareness of diverse leadership styles
- Expand knowledge base of skills and competencies for career growth
- Clarify values, goals, and choices and develop career satisfaction
- Develop better learning strategies
- Enhance entrepreneurial skills
- Improve presentation skills
- Maximize goal setting and priorities and manage time more efficiently
- Develop strategic planning skills, such as how to plan and monitor projects more effectively
- Improve delegation skills

Organizational Capabilities Solutions for Executives

- Direct and support organizational change
- Improve ability to manage an organization, for instance, strategic planning, negotiation, and problem solving
- Lead re-engineering, restructuring, or downsizing initiatives
- Increase productivity
- Strategically reposition the organization in the marketplace

APPENDIX H

Sample TPS Core Statements

Emerging Leaders

- I help emerging leaders who feel they are not taken seriously develop a professional image and style readily accepted by others.
- I help emerging leaders reach their career goals by providing them with the management tools and knowledge that are often not offered by their employers.
- I help emerging leaders gain confidence through a tailor-made program for new managers that combines skill building and individual coaching.
- I help leaders who are unsure of their plans and direction gain clarity and focus and create a solid plan of action.

Female Leaders

- I help isolated female leaders obtain a deeper connection with themselves and their teams.
- I help female leaders who are challenged by difficult conversations have productive conversations that produce breakthrough results.

- I help female leaders who "do it all" learn to trust what is theirs and what is not.
- I help female leaders who feel "is this it?" discover what may be "missing."

Leaders

- I help leaders who feel overwhelmed and disenfranchised re-anchor and re-engage with commitment, purpose, and energy.
- I help leaders who are faced with enormous change create a compelling vision for the future that they feel committed to move toward.
- I help leaders who feel unequipped in the new business climate gain the skill sets needed to innovate and motivate for future success.
- I help leaders who "do it all" learn to trust what is theirs and what is not.

Accomplished Professionals

- I help accomplished professionals experiencing chaotic change find clarity in areas where they can realize control.
- I help accomplished professionals who are at a critical career juncture find new purpose and direction.
- I help accomplished professionals who have been impacted negatively by the economy and feel burdened by financial demands develop a new mentality to gain focus and positive traction and create a simpler, quality lifestyle.
- I utilize my personal executive management experience to coach senior managers so they can achieve balance with the overwhelming list of demands made of them by their employees and their organizations.

Couples

- I help couples with communication gaps learn to communicate effectively to improve their relationship.

- I help couples unsure and excited about their future together feel confident and strengthen their bond to create a long-lasting relationship.

- I help couples who have communication gaps, who feel they have unequal stakes in their relationship, and who are uncertain about their future together find common ground and co-create a solid, long-term partnership based on trust and love.

- I help couples who argue over different goals have constructive conversations and co-create a long-term plan.

Singles

- I help people who feel unfulfilled in their relationships create ones that are satisfying.

- I help people who are settling in their relationships develop awareness of what they deserve and the confidence to stand up for it to find the relationships they truly want.

- I help people in troubled relationships work through their barriers to have healthier relationships.

- I help people in relationships who feel unfulfilled, feel they are settling, or have communication issues get clear on what they want and need to break through their relationship barriers so that they can create meaningful relationships and feel satisfied in their personal life.

Burned Out Professionals

- I help midlifers stuck in careers they don't love find work that's play.
- I help professionals on the verge of burnout reclaim their zest for life.
- I help professionals on the verge of burnout find the will to live.
- I help burned out professionals who feel trapped find an escape hatch.

Women With Health and Fitness Issues

- I help women who hate exercise start feeling great and looking good.
- I help women who are in a serious relationship with Häagen-Dazs choose healthier hook-ups.
- I help women get off the couch and find their inner supermodel.
- I help workaholics who struggle with trying to do everything do just one thing—take care of themselves.

Young Performers

- I help bright young stars overcome self-doubt to realize their dreams.
- I help dancers who struggle with confidence relax and let their talent shine through.
- I help frightened performers find the courage to get the audition and book the job.
- I help performers who are overwhelmed, fatigued, and stressed learn the habit of self-care.

Mothers

- I help mothers having difficulty juggling between work and family get more organized and manage their responsibilities effectively.
- I help mothers who feel guilty disciplining their children learn how to discipline their children effectively while maintaining a positive home environment.
- I help mothers who feel alone when dealing with a child who is suffering a loss get support and guidance and learn their role in helping their children overcome their emotional issues and help make an impact in their growth.
- I help mothers who feel self-induced pressure that they are not doing or being enough eliminate guilt as an operator in their lives.

High-Potential Females

- I help high-potential females who have not been promoted as quickly as they deserve develop leadership presence and take the next big step on the leadership path.

- I help high-potential females who are not paid commensurately with their contribution negotiate for greater equity and advancement and ask for the title and salary commensurate with their contribution and get it.

- I help high-potential females who face discrimination and harassment develop political savvy and get proficient at navigating within the corporate landscape.

- I help high-potential females who feel like outsiders be acknowledged as team players and effective leaders.

Entrepreneurs

- I help entrepreneurs who are not comfortable marketing get unstuck and reconnect with core beliefs and values.

- I help entrepreneurs who have no infrastructure expand their personal power and reach their potential.

- I help entrepreneurs who struggle to assert themselves learn how to speak up.

- I help entrepreneurs who are "lost" discover their highest truth and manifest a life lived on purpose.

APPENDIX I

Student Samples to Inspire Your Storytelling

Sample Story

"I started my career as a leader almost thirty years ago in the corporate world as an entry-level manager trainee straight out of college and was promoted through the ranks until I became one of a few female senior leaders in our company. I really surprised myself... I didn't set out to do that.

I found out early in my career that I loved leadership so I poured myself into learning all there was to know. I soon realized that leadership is an art form in itself that takes a lifetime to cultivate. I made mistakes along the way but that's how I learned and got better. It took taking some risks with myself. Now, I have strong best practices that I share with others.

My own personal journey in the corporate world took me through many major changes, including moving my family across the country three times and heading up business initiatives that required people to quickly adapt to change—sometimes, both at the same time. Although I had a lot of accomplishments, there were some setbacks, some of which were significant. All of those experiences help me relate to my clients' desire to work through periods of uncertainty and gain clarity quickly.

About a year ago, I came to a critical career juncture, and with the help of a coach, I realized that what I found the most gratifying was helping people see their potential and surprise themselves. That's when I made the decision to start a coaching practice. Not only do I now get more self-satisfaction from what I'm doing, but I also help people accelerate the changes they want to see in themselves. I can't think of a better win–win situation.

As your coach, you can expect me to help you develop inspiring goals and keep you focused and on track. I want to help you achieve your potential. You can count on me to provide a safe environment where you can try on new thinking without being judged. And you can also expect me to stretch and challenge your thinking with stimulating questions designed to help you reveal your own solutions. My goal is for you to surprise yourself!

I'm really looking forward to getting to know you better and working with you to obtain your most challenging goals."

Sample Story Pieces

What differentiates me as a coach?

- I boldly challenge my clients, while keeping it safe for them to explore new possibilities.
- I help people quickly break through limiting beliefs to move forward in life with conviction and courage.
- My coaching is integrative, exploring the coherence between emotions, language, and the body.
- My approach to coaching uniquely weaves through the mind and the heart. I combine the rigors of diverse business expertise with presence and intuition for the sake of helping clients achieve break-through results.

Why Do I Coach?

- I coach because I am passionate about helping people discover their highest human potential.
- I believe that when I coach, I truly become more of who I am.
- I coach because I get excited about possibilities from the learning.
- I coach because I love facilitating breakthrough results that surpass expectations.
- I coach because I think it is one of the greatest gifts we can offer; it is the gift of our presence to another.

What You Can Expect

- What you can expect from me is to be boldly challenged and safely supported in your growth as a leader.
- We will dance together by simply allowing the music that calls us to pace our steps. It is always there and can be accessed and trusted if we learn to listen.
- Guided by your goals, my coaching is fearless and integrated; I am passionate about achieving results.

Student Sample for What Makes Me Credible?

"We [my business partner and I] have struggled with many career issues/challenges/roadblocks. We've experienced career rejoicing and career disappointments and have learned to face it and move forward. We have both developed high-performing teams in both explosive growth and downsizing environments. [We] worked our way up, experiencing what it was like to work at all levels. We've walked in our target market's shoes. We've experienced being put in challenging situations and/or new positions before we were ready and can help people take a more direct path. We learned throughout our careers to push through when we hit a rocky patch; we learned to see the possibilities, get to acceptance, and keep moving. We sought out the best of the best mentors and paid it forward by becoming mentors to upcoming leaders. [We] dedicated our lives to learning and applying the art of leadership and have developed best practices for each level of management. We are known as developers of leaders and have over fifty-five years combined experience developing hundreds of leaders who have become very successful. As we ascended in our careers and took on broader scopes of responsibilities, we learned the value of long-term strategic planning. Our career ascension happened through hard work, teamwork, commitment, learning from our mistakes, and being intuitive."

APPENDIX J

Sample Offers

Emerging Leaders

- Free article on self-projection and image when you register with your name and email address
- Link to take a free self-assessment and receive 10% off on a teleconference series
- Sign up for a free monthly newsletter (include upcoming events)
- Free trial session for a one-on-one coaching session
- Free 1-hour leader panel call with questions submitted in advance and selected questions answered by leadership expert panel
- Free informational call on content of "real problem" teleconference series

Ascending Female Leaders

- Free self-assessment on core competencies
- Article on "Breaking Through Real and Imagined Boundaries"
- Free trial session for one-on-one coaching
- Sign up for the monthly newsletter
- Article: "How to Use Your Fire to Slow Down to the Pace of Life"

- Speak at women's conference

Accomplished Professionals

- Free trial coaching session geared toward career-guidance goal with offer of a mini-coaching series
- Free information call on "Creating Career Options," followed by an offer of a free trial coaching session
- Article on simplifying life
- Presentation on "Managing Change" or "Reinventing Self in Today's Tough Economy"
- Monthly newsletter
- Self-assessment: current satisfaction identification

For All

- Friend me on Linkedin and Facebook
- Check out my new website and tell me what you think
- "Event Ticket" for gratis teleconference

Growth and Trouble Mindset

- Gratis mini-session
- Self-assessment

Even-Keel and Over-Confident Mindset

- Article
- Stay in touch
- Get email address
- Friend me on Facebook, Linkedin, or Plaxo
- Monthly newsletter
- Check out my new website and tell me what you think

APPENDIX K

Sample Rate Packaging

We offer three packages for committed professionals who want to make positive, sustainable change in three months.

Platinum: Four 1-hour sessions at a monthly fee of $____

- 360 Degree Customized Assessment
- Unlimited calls with coach in between sessions, limited to five minutes each call
- Unlimited emailing in between sessions

Gold: Four 1-hour sessions at a monthly rate of $____

- One call per week in between sessions, limited to five minutes each call
- One email per week in between sessions

Silver: Four 30-minute sessions at a monthly rate of $____

- One call per week in between sessions, limited to five minutes each call
- One email per week in between sessions

All packages have a 100% satisfaction guarantee.

If, after the first month of coaching, you feel you are dissatisfied for any reason whatsoever, I will refund your entire fee.

APPENDIX L

Marketing Plan Template

Target Market 1: Top three strategies

1.

_____

_____

2.

_____

_____

3.

_____

_____

Tools I need for each strategy:

1.

_____

_____

2.

_____

_____

3.

_____

_____

Target Market 2: Top three strategies

1.

_____

_____

2.

_____

_____

3.

_____

_____

Tools I need for each strategy:

1.

_____

_____

2.

_____

_____

3.

_____

_____

Target Market 3: Top three strategies

   1.

_____

_____

   2.

_____

_____

   3.

_____

_____

Tools I need for each strategy:

   1.

_____

_____

   2.

_____

_____

   3.

_____

_____

APPENDIX M

Find Your Natural Marketing Style

To find out which marketing strategies are most natural and authentic for you, answer the following questions.

Making Connections and Being Known

I like to meet potential clients face-to-face in a networking type setting.

    ○ Most   ○ Least

I prefer connecting one-on-one versus a group setting.

    ○ Most   ○ Least

I feel confident in my ability to connect with others at both social and business gatherings.

    ○ Most   ○ Least

I like volunteering my services to the community.

    ○ Most   ○ Least

I need to feel connected to a team or community of like-minded professionals.

    ○ Most   ○ Least

I enjoy creating business alliances with my peers.

    ○ Most   ○ Least

Getting the Word Out

I am comfortable with using print advertising to promote my business.

    ○ Most   ○ Least

I am comfortable with the Internet.

    ○ Most   ○ Least

I prefer for others to promote my services.

    ○ Most   ○ Least

I'm comfortable with letting others know why they should recommend me.

    ○ Most   ○ Least

I feel best about using referrals, endorsements, and testimonials.

    ○ Most   ○ Least

I like and am effective at creating profiles on social media sites.

    ○ Most   ○ Least

Speaking and Presenting

I'm good at motivating people with words and calling them to action.

    ○ Most   ○ Least

I feel good about my voice quality.

    ○ Most   ○ Least

I am always happy to demonstrate my skills.

    ○ Most   ○ Least

I would like to give keynote speeches.

    ○ Most   ○ Least

I have superior presentation skills.

    ○ Most   ○ Least

I am comfortable speaking to large groups.

    ○ Most   ○ Least

I would enjoy participating in a radio show as a guest speaker or host.

    ○ Most   ○ Least

I am comfortable in front of the camera.

    ○ Most   ○ Least

I would enjoy being interviewed about what I do.

    ○ Most   ○ Least

Writing and Preparation

I'm good at explaining what I do in writing.

    ○ Most   ○ Least

I like writing and delivering curricula.

    ○ Most   ○ Least

I would enjoy creating e-zines and newsletters.

    ○ Most   ○ Least

I would enjoy creating a weekly newspaper column.

    ○ Most   ○ Least

I would love to create a blog to speak about my business.

    ○ Most   ○ Least

APPENDIX N

Top 10 Testimonial Questions by Thomas Leonard

(Excerpted with permission from www.coachville.com)

1. "What are the three important ways that you have benefited from our working together?" (Accept what they say, and then press for clarity/simplicity/truth)

2. "Have you benefited in surprising ways, perhaps outside of what you hired me to do for you?" (Press for truth/release)

3. "Is there an area of our work together that you would like to spend more time on?" (Be patient as they create this; this tells you what they want more of and may help you expand your practice by serving others with similar needs)

4. "Five years from now, what will you say about the work we have done together to this point?" (Be patient as they process this)

5. "You know me as a [insert your profession here]. What ELSE would you call me or the role I play in your life?" (Have fun with them as they think of this; press for other examples until one rings true for both of you)

6. "What are the three positive adjectives which describe me?" (This, so that you can discover how you or your personality are perceived, which you can craft into added features and benefits of your work.)

7. "What are the three ways that our working together is saving you money and/or making you more money?" (Be patient as they identify these)

8. "How is our working together improving the quality of your personal life?"(Be patient; they aren't expecting this one)

9. "As a result of our working together, what have you been freed up to do and accomplish work-wise or business-wise?" (Be patient; they need to connect the dots between you, your work, them, and their business/work)

10. "Given my goal is to identify everything that you receive/get from our working together, what else would you want to add to make this list complete?" (This is the BIG question.)

APPENDIX O

Personal Action Plan

Specific actions: *Due date for each:*

_____

_____

_____

_____

_____

_____

_____

_____

_____

_____

Obstacles I might encounter:

_____

_____

_____

_____

_____

_____

_____

Tactics for overcoming obstacles:

_____

_____

_____

_____

_____

_____

How do I hold myself accountable and keep myself moving forward?

_____

_____

_____

_____

_____

_____

_____

_____

_____

What resources can I call upon for help?

_____

_____

_____

ABOUT THE AUTHOR

PAULETTE RAO, MCC, BCC, is a leader-  ship coach, mentor coach, speaker, trainer, and marketing expert. She is the principal of True North Resources, LLC, her coaching and consulting firm where she helps executives and entrepreneurs advance their leadership skills. Her coaching is founded on three decades of experience, many as a senior leader and marketing expert. As managing director for Marsh, the world's largest risk services firm, she was one of their top one hundred female executives.

As a Master Certified Coach, Paulette works with leaders, executives, independent contributors, entrepreneurs, and teams who want to accelerate their effectiveness, sustain organizational vitality, and optimize leadership performance. She identifies and builds on existing competencies to create a bridge toward desired personal and professional outcomes and corporate strategic goals. While her work is guided by a focus on results, it's Paulette's passionate style and presence that truly resonate with her clients.

Paulette created the Conscious Coaching Institute to train and develop coaches. Here she provides various services that help coaches hone their skills and build their practice. Her OneSource™: ICF Credentialing Made Easy mentor coaching program fully supports the coach who is pursuing an ICF credential. Candidates further develop in the core competencies and are superbly positioned to pass the credentialing exam with presence and confidence.

Through her teaching at New York University, Paulette helps coaches gain the clarity and confidence needed to create compelling marketing messages and plans to attract the people they most want to work with, resulting in a sustainable practice.

At the urging of her clients and students, Paulette took her best practices as a mentor and marketing coach to create the workbook *Conscious Marketing: Marketing from the Inside Out*.

Paulette is a trainer for leading coach-training organizations specializing in bringing the benefits of a coaching approach into corporate settings to develop talent and improve performance and leadership.

She holds her Bachelor of Arts in Education. She is a founding fellow of the Harvard Institute of Professional Coaching and member of the International Positive Psychology Association.

She holds several coaching and leadership certifications: Master Certified Coach with the International Coach Federation; Board Certified Coach by the Center for Credentialing and Education, Inc. (CCE); Advanced Leadership from the Bell Institute; certified NeuroLeadership coach through NeuroLeadership Group; and certified Executive and Organizational Coach from New York University where she is a professor in the professional coaching certificate program.

Passionate about serving the coaching community, Paulette now serves on the Board of Directors for the New York City Chapter of the International Coaching Federation. She may be contacted at paulette@ truenorthresources.com, (917) 921-7852, www.truenorthresources.com